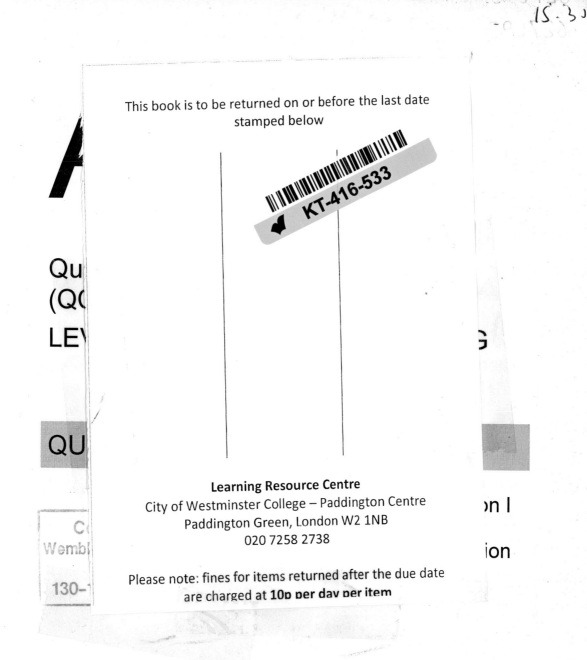

This book is to be returned on or before the last date stamped below

KT-416-533

Qu
(Q(
LE\   G

QU   ɔn I

C
Wembl   ion

130–

First edition July 2010
Third edition July 2012

ISBN 9781 4453 9486 2
(Previous edition 9780 7517 9759 6)

British Library Cataloguing-in-Publication Data
A catalogue record for this book is available from the British
Library

Published by

BPP Learning Media Ltd
BPP House
Aldine Place
London W12 8AA

www.bpp.com/learningmedia

Printed in the United Kingdom

Your learning materials, published by BPP Learning Media
Ltd, are printed on paper sourced from sustainable, managed
forests.

CONTENTS

Introduction (v)

Question and Answer bank

Chapter tasks		**Questions**	**Answers**
1	Accounting principles	3	73
2	Accounting concepts	8	78
3	Purchase of non-current assets	10	80
4	Depreciation of non-current assets	15	84
5	Disposal of non-current assets	19	88
6	Accruals and prepayments	22	91
7	Inventory	25	94
8	Irrecoverable debts and doubtful debts	28	97
9	Bank reconciliations	33	100
10	Control account reconciliations	38	103
11	The trial balance, errors and the suspense account	44	107
12	The extended trial balance	54	114
AAT practice assessment 1		127	143
AAT practice assessment 2		153	169
BPP practice assessment 1		179	191
BPP practice assessment 2		201	213
BPP practice assessment 3		223	235
BPP practice assessment 4		245	259

A NOTE ABOUT COPYRIGHT

Dear Customer

What does the little © mean and why does it matter?

Your market-leading BPP books, course materials and e-learning materials do not write and update themselves. People write them: on their own behalf or as employees of an organisation that invests in this activity. Copyright law protects their livelihoods. It does so by creating rights over the use of the content.

Breach of copyright is a form of theft – as well as being a criminal offence in some jurisdictions, it is potentially a serious breach of professional ethics.

With current technology, things might seem a bit hazy but, basically, without the express permission of BPP Learning Media:

- Photocopying our materials is a breach of copyright

- Scanning, ripcasting or conversion of our digital materials into different file formats, uploading them to Facebook or emailing them to your friends is a breach of copyright

You can, of course, sell your books, in the form in which you have bought them – once you have finished with them. (Is this fair to your fellow students? We update for a reason.)

And what about outside the UK? BPP Learning Media strives to make our materials available at prices students can afford by local printing arrangements, pricing policies and partnerships which are clearly listed on our website. A tiny minority ignore this and indulge in criminal activity by illegally photocopying our material or supporting organisations that do. If they act illegally and unethically in one area, can you really trust them?

INTRODUCTION

This is BPP Learning Media's AAT Question Bank for Accounts Preparation I. It is part of a suite of ground breaking resources produced by BPP Learning Media for the AAT's assessments under the qualification and credit framework.

The Accounts Preparation I assessment will be **computer assessed**. As well as being available in the traditional paper format, this **Question Bank is available in an online format** where all questions and assessments are presented in a **style which mimics the style of the AAT's assessments**. BPP Learning Media believe that the best way to practise for an online assessment is in an online environment. However, if you are unable to practise in the online environment you will find that all tasks in the paper Question Bank have been written in a style that is as close as possible to the style that you will be presented with in your online assessment.

This Question Bank has been written in conjunction with the BPP Text, and has been carefully designed to enable students to practise all of the learning outcomes and assessment criteria for the units that make up Accounts Preparation I. It is fully up to date as at July 2012 and reflects both the AAT's Guidance and the practice assessments provided by the AAT.

This Question Bank contains these key features:

- tasks corresponding to each chapter of the Text. Some tasks are designed for learning purposes, others are of assessment standard

- the AAT's practice assessments and answers for Accounts Preparation I

- Four further full practice assessments

The emphasis in all tasks and assessments is on the practical application of the skills acquired.

VAT

You will find tasks throughout this Question Bank which need you to calculate or be aware of a rate of VAT. This is stated at 20% in these examples and questions.

Approaching the assessment

When you sit the assessment it is very important that you follow the on screen instructions. This means you need to carefully read the instructions, both on the introduction screens and during specific tasks.

When you access the assessment you should be presented with an introductory screen with information similar to that shown below (taken from the introductory screen from one of the AAT's Practice Assessments for Accounts Preparation I).

This assessment is in TWO sections.
You must show competence in BOTH sections.
You should therefore attempt and aim to complete EVERY task in EACH section.
Each task is independent. You will not need to refer to your answers to previous tasks.
Read every task carefully to make sure you understand what is required.

Where the date is relevant, it is given in the task data.

Both minus signs and brackets can be used to indicate negative numbers UNLESS task instructions say otherwise.

The standard rate of VAT is 20%.

You must use a full stop to indicate a decimal point.
For example, write 100.57 NOT 100,57 or 100 57

You may use a comma to indicate a number in the thousands, but you don't have to.
For example, 10000 and 10,000 are both OK.

Other indicators are not compatible with the computer-marked system.

Section 1   Complete both tasks

Section 2   Complete all 6 tasks

The actual instructions will vary depending on the subject you are studying for. It is very important you read the instructions on the introductory screen and apply them in the assessment. You don't want to lose marks when you know the correct answer just because you have not entered it in the right format.

In general, the rules set out in the AAT Practice Assessments for the subject you are studying for will apply in the real assessment, but you should again read the information on this screen in the real assessment carefully just to make sure. This screen may also confirm the VAT rate used if applicable.

A full stop is needed to indicate a decimal point. We would recommend using minus signs to indicate negative numbers and leaving out the comma signs to indicate thousands, as this results in a lower number of key strokes and less margin for error when working under time pressure. Having said that, you can use whatever is easiest for you as long as you operate within the rules set out for your particular assessment.

You have to show competence in both sections of assessments and you should therefore complete all of the tasks. Don't leave questions unanswered.

In some assessments written or complex tasks may be human marked. In this case you are given a blank space or table to enter your answer into. You are told in the practice assessments which tasks these are (note: there may be none if all answers are marked by the computer).

If these involve calculations, it is a good idea to decide in advance how you are going to lay out your answers to such tasks by practising answering them on a word document, and certainly you should try all such tasks in this question bank and in the AAT's environment using the practice assessments.

When asked to fill in tables, or gaps, never leave any blank even if you are unsure of the answer. Fill in your best estimate.

Note that for some assessments where there is a lot of scenario information or tables of data provided (eg tax tables), you may need to access these via 'pop-ups'. Instructions will be provided on how you can bring up the necessary data during the assessment.

Finally, take note of any task specific instructions once you are in the assessment. For example you may be asked to enter a date in a certain format or to enter a number to a certain number of decimal places.

Remember you can practise the BPP questions in this question bank in an online environment on our dedicated AAT Online page. On the same page is a link to the current AAT Practice Assessments as well.

If you have any comments about this book, please e-mail paulsutcliffe@bpp.com or write to Paul Sutcliffe, Senior Publishing Manager, BPP Learning Media Ltd, BPP House, Aldine Place, London W12 8AA.

Question bank

Accounts Preparation I Question Bank

Chapter 1

Task 1.1

Compete the sentences below by selecting the appropriate option from the Picklist.

The sales returns day book lists...	Credit note sent to custom ▼ ✓
The purchases day book lists...	invoice received from Supplier ▼
The purchases returns day book lists...	Credit note received from ▼ Sup
The sales day book lists...	Invoice Sent to custom ▼

Picklist:

invoices sent to customers
credit notes sent to customers
invoices received from suppliers
credit notes received from suppliers

....

Task 1.2

What are the two effects of each of these transactions for accounting purposes?

Transaction	Account 1			Account 2		
	Name	Increase ✓	Decrease ✓	Name	Increase ✓	Decrease ✓
Payment of £15,000 into a business bank account by an individual in order to start up a business						
Payment by cheque of £2,000 for rent of a business property						
Payment by cheque of £6,200 for purchase of a delivery van						
Payment by cheque of £150 for vehicle licence for the van						
Payment by cheque of £2,100 for goods for resale						

3

Transaction	Account 1			Account 2		
	Name	Increase ✓	Decrease ✓	Name	Increase ✓	Decrease ✓
Sale of goods for cash and cheques of £870						
Purchase of goods for resale on credit for £2,800						
Payment by cheque for petrol of £80						
Sale of goods on credit for £3,400						
Payment by cheque of £1,500 to credit suppliers						
Payment by cheque of electricity bill of £140						
Receipt of cheque from credit customer of £1,600						
Withdrawal of £500 of cash for the owner's personal living costs						
Payment by cheque for petrol of £70						

Task 1.3

For each of the transactions in the previous activity enter the amounts into the ledger accounts given below, then balance each of the accounts and prepare a trial balance at the end of this initial period of trading.

Capital account

	£		£

Bank account

	£		£

Rent account

	£		£

Van account

	£		£

Van expenses account

	£		£

Purchases account

	£		£

Sales account

	£		£

Purchases ledger control account

	£		£

Sales ledger control account

	£		£

Electricity account

	£		£

Drawings account

	£		£

Trial balance	Debit £	Credit £
Capital		
Bank		
Rent		
Van		
Van expenses		
Purchases		
Sales		
Payables ie purchases ledger control account		
Receivables ie sales ledger control account		
Electricity		
Drawings		

Task 1.4

A credit balance on a ledger account indicates

✓	
	An asset or an expense
	A liability or an expense
	An amount owing to the organisation
	A liability or a revenue item

Chapter 2

Task 2.1

For each of the following statements determine which accounting concept is being invoked:

(a) Computer software, although for long-term use in the business, is charged to the income statement when purchased as its value is small in comparison to the hardware.

Concept	

(b) The non-current assets of the business are valued at their carrying amount rather than the value for which they might be sold.

Concept	

(c) The expenses that the business incurs during the year are charged as expenses in the income statement even if the amount of the expense has not yet been paid in cash.

Concept	

Task 2.2

The two fundamental accounting concepts are

	and	

Task 2.3

Classify the following items as long-term assets ('non-current assets'), short-term assets ('current assets') or liabilities.

	Non-current assets ✓	Current assets ✓	Liabilities ✓
A PC used in the accounts department of a retail store			
A PC on sale in an office equipment shop			
Wages due to be paid to staff at the end of the week			
A van for sale in a motor dealer's showroom			
A delivery van used in a grocer's business			
An amount owing to a bank for a loan for the acquisition of a van, to be repaid over 9 months			

Task 2.4

Which of the following best explains what is meant by 'capital expenditure'?

Capital expenditure is expenditure:

✓	
	On non-current assets, including repairs and maintenance
	On expensive assets
	Relating to the acquisition or improvement of non-current assets
	Incurred by the chief officer of the business

Chapter 3

Task 3.1

In each of the following circumstances determine how much capital expenditure has been incurred and how much revenue expenditure has been incurred by a business that is registered for VAT:

	Capital expenditure £	Revenue expenditure £
An SN63 sanding machine has been purchased at a cost of £12,000 plus VAT. The delivery charge was £400. After its initial run it was cleaned at a cost of £100.		
A building has been purchased at a cost of £120,000. The surveyor's fees were an additional £400 and the legal fees £1,200. The building has been re-decorated at a total cost of £13,000.		
A new main server has been purchased at a cost of £10,600. In order to house the server a room in the building has had to have a special air conditioning unit fitted at a cost of £2,450. The server's cost includes software worth £1,000 and CDs with a value of £100.		
A salesperson's car has been purchased at a cost of £14,000 plus VAT. The invoice also shows delivery costs of £50 (inclusive of VAT) and road fund licence of £160 (no VAT charged). The car is available for private use by the salesperson.		

Task 3.2

A business has just spent money on two of its machines. The SPK100 has been repaired after a breakdown at a cost of £2,400. The FL11 has had a new engine fitted at a cost of £3,100 which it is anticipated will extend its useful life to the business by four years.

The SPK100 repairs would be treated as

✓	
	capital expenditure
	revenue expenditure

The FL11 repairs would be treated as

✓	
	capital expenditure
	revenue expenditure

....

Task 3.3

Draft journal entries for each of the following transactions by a business that is registered for VAT:

(a) Purchase of a salesperson's car for £12,000 plus VAT and road fund licence of £150 paid for by cheques.

	Debit £	Credit £
Motor vehicles account		
Motor expenses account		
Bank account		

(b) Purchase of a machine for £15,400 plus VAT, on credit, and the alterations to the factory floor required that used employees' labour with a wage cost of £1,400.

	Debit £	Credit £
Machinery account		
VAT account		
Purchases ledger control account		
Wages account		

(c) Purchase of a computer for £3,800 plus VAT by cheque which included £100 of printer paper and £50 of CDs.

	Debit £	Credit £
Computer account		
Computer expenses account		
VAT account		
Bank account		

(d) Redecorating of the room which houses the computer prior to its installation, £800 paid by cheque. Ignore VAT.

	Debit £	Credit £
Building maintenance account		
Bank account		

(e) Insurance of the new computer was paid by cheque of £200. Ignore VAT.

	Debit £	Credit £
Computer expenses account		
Bank account		

Task 3.4

Write up the following transactions in the ledger accounts given:

(a) A machine was purchased for £13,500 plus VAT by cheque and installed using the business's own employees at a wage cost of £400 and own materials at a cost of £850.

(b) A building was purchased for £150,000 plus £20,000 of alterations in order to make it of use to the business. The unaltered parts of the building were then redecorated at a cost of £4,000. All purchases were paid for by cheque. Ignore VAT.

Machinery account

	£		£
Balance b/d	103,400.00		

Buildings account

	£		£
Balance b/d	200,000.00		

VAT account

	£		£
		Balance b/d	13,289.60

Purchases account

	£		£
Balance b/d	56,789.50		

Wages account

	£		£
Balance b/d	113,265.88		

Buildings maintenance account

	£		£
Balance b/d	10,357.00		

Bank account

	£		£
Balance b/d	214,193.60		

Task 3.5

When a business uses its own work force to install some non-current assets, the cost of the labour may be added to the cost of the non-current asset.

✓	
	True
	False

Task 3.6

Which of the following costs would be classified as capital expenditure for a restaurant business?

✓	
	A replacement for a broken window
	Repainting the restaurant
	An illuminated sign advertising the business name
	Knives and forks for the restaurant

Chapter 4

Task 4.1

The accounting concept that underlies the charging of depreciation is

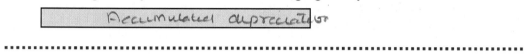

Accumulated depreciation

....

Task 4.2

Calculate the depreciation charge using the straight line method for each of the following non-current assets for the year ended 31 December 20X8. Also calculate the carrying amount of each asset at 31 December 20X8:

	Workings	Depreciation charge £	Carrying amount £
Machine purchased for £17,400 on 1 January 20X6 with a useful life of 5 years and a zero residual value.	17,400 ÷ 5 = 3480 3×3480	3480	16960
Machine purchased for £12,800 on 1 January 20X7 with a useful life of 4 years and a residual value of £2,000.	12,80 ÷ 4 = 9700 2×9700	2700	7400
Computer purchased for £4,600 on 1 January 20X8 with a useful life of 3 years and an estimated resale value of £700.	4600/3 = 1533 4600-1533	1533	3067

....

1533   10440   5400

7400

[handwritten top:] $3800 \times \frac{30}{100} = 1140 \ (2660)$
$2660 \times \frac{30}{100} = 798 \ (1862)$

Task 4.3

For each of the following non-current assets calculate the depreciation charge for the year ended 31 March 20X9 and the carrying amount at 31 March 20X9:

	Workings	Depreciation charge £	Carrying amount £
Machinery costing £24,600 purchased on 1 April 20X8 which is to be depreciated at 20% on the reducing balance basis.	$24600 \times \frac{20}{100}$ $= 4920$	4920	19680
Motor vehicle costing £18,700 purchased on 1 April 20X6 which is to be depreciated at 20% on the reducing balance basis.	$18700 \times \frac{20}{100}$ $= 3740$	2394	9574
Computer costing £3,800 purchased on 1 April 20X7 which is to be depreciated at 30% on the reducing balance basis.	$3800 \times 3\%/100$	798	1862

[handwritten:] $18700 - 3740 = 14960$ ①
$14960 \times \frac{20}{100} = 2992 \ (11968)$ ②
$11968 \times 20/100 = 2394 \ (9574)$ ③

Task 4.4

Calculate the depreciation charge for the year ended 31 December 20X8 for each of the following non-current assets:

	Workings	Depreciation charge £
Machine purchased on 1 May 20X8 for £14,000. This is to be depreciated at the rate of 20% per annum on the straight-line basis. Depreciation is calculated on an annual basis and charged in equal instalments for each full month an asset is owned in the year.	$14000 \times \frac{20}{100}$ $= 2800 \times \frac{8}{12}$	1867
Office furniture and fittings purchased on 1 June 20X8 for £3,200. These are to be depreciated on the reducing balance basis at a rate of 25% with a full year's charge in the year of purchase and no charge in the year of disposal.	$3200 \times \frac{25}{100}$ 800	800
Computer purchased on 31 October 20X8 for £4,400. This is to be depreciated at the rate of 40% per annum on the straight-line basis. Depreciation is calculated on an annual basis and charged in equal instalments for each full month an asset is owned in the year.	$4,400 \times \frac{40}{100}$ $= 1760 \times \frac{2}{12}$	293

Task 4.5

On 1 January 20X0 a business purchased a laser printer costing £1,800. What are the annual depreciation charges for the accounting years ended 31 December 20X0, 20X1, 20X2 and 20X3 on the laser printer if the reducing balance method is used at 60% per annum?

Note. Your workings should be to the nearest £.

	Workings	Depreciation charge £
20X0		1080
20X1		432
20X2		173
20X3		69

Task 4.6

What is the double entry for a depreciation charge for the accounting period?

Debit	depreciation charge
Credit	Accumulated depreciation

Task 4.7

A machine was purchased for £2,800 on 1 July 20X4. The depreciation policy is to depreciate machinery on a reducing balance basis at 40% per annum with a full year's charge in the year of purchase and no charge in the year of disposal. The business year end is 31 December.

1120

What is the carrying amount of the machine at 31 December 20X7 (round to the nearest £)?

	✓	
	✓	£605
		£363
		£179
		£72

Task 4.8

What is the purpose of accounting for depreciation in financial statements?

✓	
✓	To allocate the cost less residual value of a non-current asset over the accounting periods expected to benefit from its use
	To ensure that funds are available for the eventual replacement of the asset
	To reduce the cost of the asset to its estimated market value
	To recognise the fact that assets lose their value over time

Chapter 5

Task 5.1

A non-current asset was purchased on 1 April 20X7 for £12,500 and is being depreciated at 30% per annum on the reducing balance basis, with a full year's charge in the year of disposal. On 31 March 20X9 the asset was sold for £6,000.

What is the profit or loss on the sale of the non-current asset?

profit/loss	of £	*125*

Task 5.2

A non-current asset was purchased on 1 January 20X6 for £25,000. It is being depreciated over its useful life of 5 years on the straight-line basis with a residual value of £3,000 and a full year's charge in the year of disposal. The asset was sold on 31 December 20X8 for £11,000.

Show the accounting entries for this asset from the day of purchase to the day of sale in the following ledger accounts. The business has a statement of financial position date of 31 December each year.

Non-current asset at cost account

	£		£
asset	*25,000*	*Disposal*	*9500*

Depreciation account

	£		£
Acc dep·	*13200*	*SPL*	*13200*

Accumulated depreciation account

	£		£
disposal	*13200*	*dep char*	*13200*

BPP
LEARNING MEDIA

Disarrangement account

Disposal account

	£		£
Asset	25,000	Acc dep –	13,200
		Bank	11,000
		SPL Loss –	800
	25,000		25,200

1 April 20X7 — 31 Mar 20X8
1 April 20X8 ⊂ 31 Mar 2009

Task 5.3

A motor vehicle had been purchased on 1 April 20X7 for £13,800 and has been depreciated on the reducing balance basis at a rate of 30% per annum. It was sold on 31 March 20X9 for £7,000.

You are required to write up the ledger accounts for the year ended 31 March 20X9 to reflect the ownership and sale of this motor vehicle. A full year's charge for depreciation is to be charged in the year of disposal.

Depreciation expense account

		£			£
20X8					
31 March Acc dep 2009		4140	SPL –		4140
31 March		2898	SPL		2898

Accumulated depreciation account

		£	2009		£
31 March 2009 Bal c/d		7038	1 April 2008		4140
			31 March 2009 –		2898
		7038			7038
			Bal b/d		7038
					7038

Motor vehicle at cost account

1 April 2008	£	31 Dec	£
Cost at asset	13,800	disposal	13,800

Disposal account

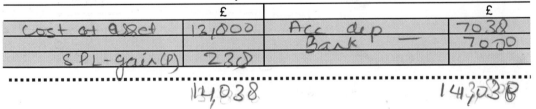

	£		£
Cost of asset	13,000	Acc dep –	7038
SPL – gain (P)	238	Bank –	7000
	14,038		14,038

Task 5.4

A machine was purchased on 30 June 20X6 for £15,600. The depreciation policy is to depreciate this asset at a rate of 25% per annum on a straight line basis. Depreciation is calculated on an annual basis and charged in equal instalments for each full month an asset is owned in the year. On 30 November 20X8 the machine was sold for £6,000. The business has an accounting year ending 31 December.

Write up the disposal account to reflect the disposal of this asset.

Disposal account

	£		£
Cost at asset	15,600	Acc dep	9425
		Bank -	6000
		SPL - Loss	175
	15600		15,600

15425

Task 5.5

Your firm bought a machine for £5,000 on 1 January 20X1, which had an expected useful life of four years and an expected residual value of £1,000. Depreciation is on a straight line basis. On 31 December 20X3 the machine was sold for £1,600.

The amount to be entered in the 20X3 income statement on disposal is

✓	
	Profit of £600
	Loss of £600
	Profit of £350
✓	Loss of £400

$$5000X \quad \frac{5000 - 1000}{4} = \frac{4000}{4} \quad 1000 \times 3 = 3000$$

5000 - 3000
Carrying = 2000
amount
Sold - 1600 = 400 Loss

Chapter 6

Task 6.1

During the year ended 31 March a business has paid £845 of telephone bills. However the bill for February and March has not been received and is expected to be approximately £170.

You are required to write up the following ledger account to reflect the telephone expense for the year showing the charge to the income statement for the year.

Telephone account

	£		£
Bank -	845	S PL -	1015
Accrued exp -	170		
	1615		

Task 6.2

Given below is the electricity expense account for the year ended 30 June for a business. At 30 June it is estimated from meter readings that the electricity bill for the final three months of the accounting year will be £900. The bill for £900 is eventually received and paid on 21 July.

You are required to write up the following ledger account showing the year end accrual and the charge to the income statement for the year.

Electricity account

	£		£
30 June Bank	2,300	SPL —	3200
Accrued e/	900		
	3200		

Task 6.3

The cash payments book for a business shows that in the year ended 31 May 20X8 £2,300 was paid for insurance. However this includes £250 for the year ending 31 May 20X9.

You are required to write up the insurance account to reflect this and to show the charge to the income statement for the year.

Insurance account

	£	Balc /cl	£
31 May Bank	2,300	Prepaid Insuran	250
		SPI —	2050
	2300		2300

Task 6.4

A business pays rent for its premises in advance. The rent expense account for the year ending 30 June is given below but of this expense £400 is for the month of July.

You are required to write up the rent account to reflect this and to show the income statement charge for the year.

Rent account

	£		£
30 June Bank	4,500	Prepaid Expens	400
		SPL	4100
	4500		4500

Task 6.5

A business sublets some of its premises to tenants who pay in advance. The rental income account for the year to 30 June is given below. £5,600 is received during the year of which £350 is in advance for the following month.

You are required to show the entries required in the rental income ledger account including the income statement income figure for the year to 30 June.

Rental income account

	£		£

Task 6.6

An electricity accrual of £375 was treated as a prepayment in preparing a business's income statement for the year ended 31 December 20X4.

What was the resulting effect on the electricity expense of the business for the year?

	✓	
		Overstated by £375
		Overstated by £750
	✓	Understated by £375
	✓	Understated by £750

Task 6.7

Cleverley Ltd started in business on 1 January 20X0, preparing accounts to 31 December 20X0. The electricity bills received were as follows.

		£
30 April 20X0	For 4 months to 30 April 20X0	5,279.47
31 July 20X0	For 3 months to 31 July 20X0	4,663.80
31 October 20X0	For 3 months to 31 October 20X0	4,117.28
31 January 20X1	For 3 months to 31 January 20X0	6,491.52

What should the electricity charge be for the year ended 31 December 20X0?

£  10388.20

Task 6.8

At 31 December 20X0 the accounts of a business show accrued rent payable of £250. During 20X1 the business pays rent bills totalling £1,275, including one bill for £375 in respect of the quarter ending 31 January 20X2.

What is the income statement charge for rent payable for the year ended 31 December 20X1?

£ 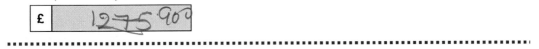 1275.90

Task 6.9

During the year £5,000 rent was received. At the beginning of the year the tenant owed £1,000 and at the end of the year the tenant owed £500.

What was the rent received figure in the year's income statement?

✓	
	£4,000
✓	£4,500
	£5,000
	£5,500

BPP LEARNING MEDIA

Chapter 7

Task 7.1

A business has 125 units of a product in inventory which cost £24.60 per unit plus £0.50 per unit of delivery costs. These goods can be sold for £25.80 per unit although in order to do this selling costs of £1.00 per unit must be incurred.

What is the cost of these units?

£

What is their net realisable value?

£

At what value will the 125 units of the product be included in the extended trial balance?

£

Task 7.2

A business has five lines of inventory. You are required to complete the table showing the value per unit for each line of the inventory and the total value to appear in the financial statements for this inventory.

Inventory line	Quantity – units	Cost £	Selling price £	Selling costs £	Value per unit £	Total value £
A	180	12.50	20.40	0.50		
B	240	10.90	12.60	1.80		
C	300	15.40	22.70	1.20		
D	80	16.50	17.80	1.50		
E	130	10.60	18.00	1.00		_____
						_____

Task 7.3

Given below are the movements on a line of inventory for the month of March:

1 Mar	Opening balance	80 units @ £8.20
7 Mar	Purchases	100 units @ £8.50
10 Mar	Sales	140 units
15 Mar	Purchases	180 units @ £8.70
26 Mar	Sales	100 units
31 Mar	Sales	70 units

What is the value of the closing inventory at 31 March using;

		£
(a)	the FIFO method	
(b)	the AVCO method	

Task 7.4

The rule for inventory is that it should be valued at

Task 7.5

Dean Ltd's inventory includes three items for which the following details are available.

	Supplier's list price £	Net realisable value £
Product A	3,600	5,100
Product B	2,900	2,800
Product C	4,200	4,100
	10,700	12,000

The business receives a 2½% trade discount from its suppliers and it also takes advantage of a 2% discount for prompt payment.

What is the value of inventory to be shown in the statement of financial position?

£

Task 7.6

In relation to inventory, net realisable value means?

✓	
	The expected selling price of the inventory
	The expected selling price less disposal costs
	The replacement cost of the inventory
	The market price

Chapter 8

Task 8.1

A business which is not registered for VAT has receivables at the year end of £5,479. Of these it has been decided that £321 from G Simms & Co will never be received as this business has now gone into liquidation. A further debt for £124 from L Fitzgerald is also viewed as irrecoverable as L Fitzgerald cannot be traced and the debt is now 8 months overdue.

You are required to write off these irrecoverable debts in the general and sales ledger accounts given below showing any charge to the income statement and the amended year end balances.

General ledger

Sales ledger control account

	£		£
Balance b/d	5,479		
		Bad irrec -	*445*
		Bal c/d -	*5034*
	5479		*5479*

Irrecoverable debts expense account

	£		£
SLCA	*445*	*SPL -*	*445*

Sales ledger

G Simms & Co

	£		£
SLCA	*321*	*Irrecoverable*	*321*

L Fitzgerald

	£		£
SLCA	*124*	*Irrecoverable*	*124*

BPP
LEARNING MEDIA

Task 8.2

A business which is registered for VAT has receivables of £16,475 at its year end of 30 September 20X8. The business's normal terms of trade are that payment from receivables is due within 30 days. On the basis of this it has been decided that two debts are to be written off as irrecoverable at the year end:

- £1,200 due from H Maguire
- £470 due from J Palmer

You are required to write off these irrecoverable debts in the general and sales ledger accounts given below showing any amounts to be charged to the income statement for the year and the amended year end balances.

General ledger

Sales ledger control account

	£		£

Irrecoverable debts expense account

	£		£

Sales ledger

H Maguire

	£		£

J Palmer

	£		£

Task 8.3

In the year ended 31 December 20X7 a business wrote off a debt for £488 owed by one of its customers, R Trevor, as irrecoverable. At 31 December 20X8 the balance on its sales ledger control account was £7,264. Of this it was decided that a debt from E Ingham for £669 would be written off as irrecoverable. In the year to 31 December 20X8 the £488 from R Trevor was unexpectedly received.

You are required to write up the general and sales ledger accounts given below for the year ended 31 December 20X8 to reflect these facts.

General ledger

Sales ledger control account

	£		£

Irrecoverable debts expense account

	£		£

Sales ledger

R Trevor

	£		£

E Ingham

	£		£

Task 8.4

Marcham has a balance on the sales ledger control account as at 30 September 20X8 of £218,940. Marcham has identified that Hendrick will not be able to pay his balance of £2,440, and wishes to write this amount off. For the remaining receivables as at 30 September 20X8, Marcham wants to have an allowance for doubtful debts of 3% of the balance. At 1 October 20X7 Marcham's allowance for doubtful debts was £5,215.

Complete the sales ledger control account, the allowance for doubtful debts account, the irrecoverable debts expense account and the allowance for doubtful debts adjustment account, closing off the expense accounts to the income statement and carrying down the balances on the statement of financial position accounts.

Sales ledger control account

	£		£

Allowance for doubtful debts account

	£		£

Irrecoverable debts expense account

	£		£

Allowance for doubtful debts adjustment account

	£		£

Task 8.5

An allowance for doubtful debts is an example of which accounting concept?

✓	
	Accruals
	Consistency
	Materiality
	Prudence

Chapter 9

Task 9.1

Albert has compared his cash book to the business bank statement for the month of May. He has identified a number of differences.

Prepare journal entries for the general ledger accounts or a note stating how it will be treated in the bank reconciliation statement, which ever is appropriate, for each of these items.

(a) Cheque number 10752, payable to a credit supplier, for £360 has been incorrectly entered in the cash book as £340.

Account name	Amount £	Debit (✓)	Credit (✓)
PLCA	20	✗	
Bank	20		✓

or

Note for bank reconciliation:

(b) Bank interest received on the bank statement of £45.

Account name	Amount £	Debit (✓)	Credit (✓)
Bank interest	45	45	
Bank statem	45		45

or

Note for bank reconciliation:

(c) A BACs receipt from a customer for £5,400 has not been entered in the cash

Account name	Amount £	Debit (✓)	Credit (✓)
Bank	5400	✓	
SLCA	5400		✓

or

Note for bank reconciliation:

(d) Cheque number 10810 for £2,356 issued on 29 May, in respect of payment of an invoice for accountancy services, is not showing on the bank statement.

Account name	Amount £	Debit (✓)	Credit (✓)
~~Cheque Bank~~	2,356		✓
PLCA	2,356	✓	

or

Note for bank reconciliation:

Task 9.2

The following differences have been identified when reconciling the cash book to the bank statement for the month of June:

1 Bank charges of £25 were not entered in the cash book.

2 The bank made an error and processed a standing order for £500 which does not relate to the business.

3 A cheque received from a credit customer for £895 has been incorrectly entered in the cash book as £859

4 A cheque received from a customer for £650, which was recorded in the cash book and paid into the bank on 30 June, is not showing on the bank statement.

Use the following table to show the adjustments, if any, you need to make to the general ledger to deal with the above differences.

Adjustment	Amount £	Debit ✓	Credit ✓
① Bank charges	25	✓	
Bank	25		✓
③ SLCA	36		✓
Bank	36	✓	

Task 9.3

Murrays Office Supplies' cash receipts and payments books for the week ending 7 July, the bank statement for that week and the bank reconciliation statement that was prepared for the week ended 30 June are set out below.

You are required to prepare the bank reconciliation statement for the week ending 7 July.

Bank reconciliation as at 7 July

	£
Balance per bank statement	
Add:	
Total to add:	
Less:	
Total to subtract:	
Balance as per cash book	

Cash Receipts Book

Date	Details	£
3 July	F Hald & Co	8,590.61
5 July	S Rose	485.21
5 July	W Field Suppliers	720.15
5 July	T Woods Manufacturing Ltd	6,351.25
6 July	R Forge	225.63
		16,372.85

Cash Payments Book

Date	Details	Cheque number	£
3 July	F W Stationers	003125	7,565.56
	A Ross & Co	003126	126.89
4 July	S Accountancy services	003127	500.00
	Grange Ltd	003128	896.78
	Wombat Supplies	003129	663.14
	Gas Suppliers	DD	1,100.00
5 July	Manor Garage	003130	105.45
7 July	Oberon Marketing	003131	4,325.00
			15,282.82

MAPLES BANK

19 Maple Square, Wallage, WA9 9PO

STATEMENT

Account Name:

Murrays Office Supplies

Account No: 71-20-21 85963245

Date	Details	DEBITS (Payments)	CREDITS (Receipts)	Balance
		£	£	£
1/7	Balance b/d			8,751.23 CR
3/7	Credit		2,875.45	11,626.68 CR
4/7	DD - Gas	1,100.00		10,526.68 CR
5/7	Cheque 3122	4,895.36		5,631.32 CR
6/7	BGC		6,351.25	
6/7	Cheque 3123	158.96		
6/7	Cheque 3125	7,565.56		4,258.05 CR
7/7	Credit		8,590.61	12,848.66 CR

Bank reconciliation statement at 30 June

	£	£
Balance per bank statement at 30 June		8,751.23
Less: unpresented cheques		
003122	4,895.36	
003123	158.96	
003124	589.45	
		(5,643.77)
		3,107.46
Add: outstanding lodgement		2,875.45
Balance as per cash book at 30 June		5,982.91

Task 9.4

Which of the following is not a valid reason for the cash book balance and the bank statement balance failing to agree?

✓	
	Timing difference
	Bank charges
	Error
	Cash receipts total posted to purchases ledger control account

Chapter 10

Task 10.1

Given below are summaries of transactions with receivables for the month of February for a business. The balance on the sales ledger control account at 1 February was £4,268.

	£
Credit sales	15,487
Sales returns	995
Irrecoverable debt written off	210
Cheques from receivables	13,486
Discounts allowed	408
Contra entry	150
Cheque returned 'refer to drawer'	645

You are required to write up the sales ledger control account showing the balance on 28 February.

Sales ledger control account

	£		£

Task 10.2

The balance on the purchases ledger control account for a business at 1 February was £3,299. The transactions with payables for the month of February are summarised below:

	£
Credit purchases	12,376
Cheques to payables	10,379
Returns to suppliers	1,074
Discounts received	302
Contra entry	230

You are required to write up the purchases ledger control account for the month and to show the closing balance on 28 February.

Purchases ledger control account

	£		£

Task 10.3

Given below is a summary of a business's transactions with its receivables and payables during the month of May. The balances on the sales ledger and purchases ledger control accounts on 1 May were £12,634 and £10,553 respectively.

	£
Credit purchases	40,375
Credit sales	51,376
Cheques from customers	50,375
Discounts received	1,245
Sales returns	3,173
Cheques to suppliers	35,795
Purchases returns	2,003
Contra entry	630
Discounts allowed	1,569

You are required to write up the sales ledger and purchases ledger control accounts for the month of May showing the balances at the end of the month.

Sales ledger control account

	£		£

Purchases ledger control account

	£		£

Task 10.4

At 31 March the balance on a business's sales ledger control account was £6,237 but the total of the list of balances from the sales ledger was £8,210. The following errors were discovered:

(a) the sales day book had been undercast by £1,000

(b) the discounts allowed of £340 had been entered into the general ledger as £430

(c) a contra entry of £123 had been made in the general ledger but not in the sales ledger

(d) a credit note to a customer for £320 had been entered on the wrong side of the customer's account in the sales ledger

(e) a credit balance of £60 had been included in the list of balances as a debit

Use the following table to show the adjustments you need to make to the sales ledger control account.

Adjustment	Amount £	Debit ✓	Credit ✓
(a)	1000	✓	
(b)	90	✓	✓
d	610		

Task 10.5

The balance on a business's purchases ledger control account at 31 January was £3,105 but the total of the list of balances from the purchases ledger was £1,850 at the same date. The following errors were discovered:

(a) the total from the purchases returns day book of £288 was entered on the wrong side of the control account

(b) a contra entry for £169 was entered in the individual supplier's account but not in the general ledger

(c) a purchase invoice for £350 was entered on the wrong side of the supplier's account in the purchases ledger

(d) the total of the cash payments book was overcast by £100

(e) a credit note to F Miller for £97 was entered into the account for A Miller

(f) a balance of £780 was incorrectly listed as £870 when the purchases ledger balances were being totalled

Use the following table to show the adjustments you need to make to the purchases ledger control account.

Adjustment	Amount £	Debit ✓	Credit ✓

Task 10.6

An investigation reveals the following errors in a business's ledgers and day books.

(i) The invoice totals for the sales day book for January was overcast by £900.00.

(ii) One invoice for £1,440.00 including VAT was duplicated in the sales day book for January.

(iii) Cash received of £120.00 from Nelson Ltd was posted to the wrong side of its sales ledger account.

(iv) The despatch column of the purchase day book for January was undercast by £270.00.

(v) One marketing invoice total for £872.00 including VAT was omitted from the purchase day book in January.

(vi) An invoice totalling £1,092.35 was posted twice to the purchases ledger account of Harrier Ltd.

(vii) A contra of £582.45 was made in the sales and purchases ledger accounts of Tremayne Holdings plc.

You are required to prepare journals to correct the general ledger accounts fully.

Account name	Debit	Credit
	£	£
Being correction of errors in sales ledger control account		
Being correction of errors in purchases ledger control account		

Task 10.7

The total of the balances in a business's sales ledger is £1,000 more than the debit balance on its sales ledger control account.

Which one of the following errors could by itself account for the discrepancy?

✓	
	The sales day book has been undercast by £1,000
	Settlement discounts totalling £1,000 have been omitted from the general ledger
	One sales ledger account with a credit balance of £1,000 has been treated as a debit balance
	The cash receipts book has been undercast by £1,000

Task 10.8

When reconciling the purchases ledger control account to the list of balances on the purchases ledger, it was discovered that an invoice received from a supplier for £72 had been recorded in the purchases day book as £27.

What adjustment is necessary to the control account and the list of balances?

✓	Control account	List of balances
	Debit £45	Add £45
	Credit £45	Add £45
	Debit £45	Subtract £45
	Credit £45	Subtract £45

Task 10.9

What is the correct treatment of discounts allowed and discounts received?

✓	Control account	List of balances
	Debit purchases ledger control	Credit sales ledger control
	Credit purchases ledger control	Credit sales ledger control
	Debit sales ledger control	Credit purchases ledger control
	Credit sales ledger control	Debit purchases ledger control

Chapter 11

Task 11.1

For each of the following errors indicate whether there is an imbalance in the trial balance or not.

Error	Imbalance ✓	No imbalance ✓
The payment of the telephone bill was posted to the cash payments book and then credited to the telephone account		
The depreciation expense was debited to the accumulated depreciation account and credited to the depreciation expense account		
The electricity account balance of £750 was taken to the trial balance as £570		
The motor expenses were debited to the motor vehicles at cost account		
The discounts received in the cash payments book were not posted to the general ledger		

Task 11.2

A trial balance has been prepared for a business and the total of the debit balances is £228,678 and the total of the credits is £220,374.

What is the balance on the suspense account?

	Debit balance ✓	Credit balance ✓
£		

Task 11.3

Draft a journal entry to correct each of the following errors – narratives should be included.

(a) The telephone expense of £236 was debited to the electricity account

Account name	Debit £	Credit £

(b) A sales invoice for £645 was entered into the sales day book as £465

Account name	Debit £	Credit £

(c) A credit note received from a supplier for £38 was omitted from the purchases returns day book

Account name	Debit £	Credit £

(d) The increase in allowance for doubtful debts of £127 was debited to the allowance for doubtful debts account and credited to the allowance for doubtful debts adjustment account

Account name	Debit £	Credit £

(e) A contra entry of £200 was debited to the sales ledger control account and credited to the purchases ledger control account

Account name	Debit £	Credit £

···

Task 11.4

A business has just drafted its trial balance and the debit balances exceed the credit balances by £1,370. A suspense account has been set up to record the difference and the following errors have been noted:

(a) The discounts allowed from the cash receipts book of £240 have not been posted to the general ledger

(b) The sales ledger column in the cash receipts book totalling £2,700 were not posted to the sales ledger control account

(c) The wages account balance of £74,275 was included in the trial balance as £72,475

(d) An irrecoverable debt written off for £235 was debited to the sales ledger control account and debited to the irrecoverable debts expense account

(e) A purchase invoice for £480 was entered into the purchases day book as £580

You are required to set up the suspense account balance and then to clear it.

Suspense account

	£		£

···

Task 11.5

When drawing up the trial balance at the end of the accounting year a suspense account debit balance of £3,100 was set up to account for the difference in the trial balance. The following errors were discovered:

(a) The payment of insurance premiums of £1,585 was correctly entered into the cash payments book and then credited to the insurance account.

(b) A payment for postage costs of £26 was posted from the petty cash book to the postage account as £62.

(c) The total of the discounts allowed column in the cash receipts book was undercast by £100.

(d) The balance of £34 on the bank interest received account was omitted from the trial balance.

(e) One page of the purchases returns day book totalling £130 was not posted to the general ledger.

You are required to set up the suspense account and then show how it is cleared.

Suspense account

	£		£

Task 11.6

Shortly before the year end a business sold a non-current asset for £4,000. The bookkeeper entered the receipt in the cash receipts book but did not know what else to do and therefore credited a suspense account with the amount. The non-current asset sold had originally cost £15,000 and had accumulated depreciation charged to it at the date of sale of £10,500.

You are to draft a journal entry to correctly account for this disposal and to show how the suspense account is cleared.

Account name	Debit £	Credit £

Task 11.7

Refer to the information provided below, and prepare a journal to clear the Green Bottles Ltd's suspense account on which there is a credit balance of £1,641.38.

(i) The balance of £43,529.18 brought down on the wages ledger account was miscast. The correct balance is £43,259.18

(ii) The balance of £25,131.14 brought down on the purchases ledger control account was miscast. The correct balance is £25,311.14

(iii) Cash received of £891.20 from Lewis & Co was posted to the wrong side of its sales ledger account

(iv) One receipt for £1,191.38 was included in the cash book in March but was omitted from the total posted to the sales ledger control account

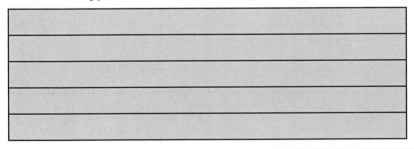

Account name	Debit £	Credit £

Task 11.8

List five different types of error in accounting transactions.

Task 11.9

When a trial balance was prepared, two ledger accounts were omitted.

Discounts received   £1,500

Discounts allowed   £1,000

The total of debit balances in the TB therefore | exceeds/falls below | **the total of credit balances by**

£	

Task 11.10

When a trial balance was prepared, a suspense account was opened. It was discovered that the only error that had been made was to record £350 of discounts received on the wrong side of the trial balance.

What is the journal to correct this error?

✓			
	Debit	Discounts received	£350
	Credit	Suspense	£350
	Debit	Suspense	£350
	Credit	Discounts received	£350
	Debit	Discounts received	£700
	Credit	Suspense	£700
	Debit	Suspense	£700
	Credit	Discounts received	£700

Task 11.11

A sole trader has drafted his initial trial balance and found that the balance on the rent account is a debit of £3,600 and the balance on the insurance account is a debit of £4,250. Rent of £1,200 is due to be paid for the final quarter of the year and the insurance payments include £850 which relate to the following accounting period.

Write in the income statement charges for:

	£
Rent	
Insurance	

Task 11.12

Given below is the initial trial balance of a sole trader for his year ended 30 June 20X8.

	Debit £	Credit £
Administration expenses	7,250	
Cash at bank	3,280	
Capital		60,000
Distribution expenses	1,210	
Purchases ledger control		1,530
Sales ledger control	20,200	
Discounts allowed	16,840	
Discounts received		
Drawings	14,600	
Machinery at cost	58,400	
Motor vehicles at cost	22,100	
Purchases	105,040	
Allowance for doubtful debts		300
Accumulated depreciation - machinery		23,360
- motor vehicles		9,680
Sales		186,070
Inventory at 1 July 20X7	15,400	
Selling expenses	5,800	
VAT owed to HMRC		3,690
Wages	16,700	
Suspense		330
	286,820	286,820

Since drawing up the initial trial balance a number of errors have been discovered:

(i) Selling expenses of £340 paid by cheque have been omitted from the accounts completely.

(ii) Purchases of £180 were entered on the wrong side of the account although the entry to the bank account was correctly made.

(iii) Discounts allowed of £690 were credited to receivables and debited to both the discounts allowed account and the discounts received account.

There are also a number of year end adjustments which have yet to be accounted for:

(iv) The closing inventory at 30 June 20X8 has been valued at £18,200.

(v) An irrecoverable debt of £2,800 is to be written off and an allowance of 2% is to be maintained of the remaining receivables.

(vi) Invoices for administration expenses for June 20X8 totalling £680 were not received until after the trial balance had been drawn up.

(vii) Included in administration expenses are payments of £440 which relate to the period after 30 June 20X8.

(viii) Depreciation has not yet been charged for the year. The machinery is depreciated at 20% per annum straight line and the motor vehicles are depreciated on the reducing balance basis at a rate of 25%.

You are required to draft journal entries to correct the errors found and put through the year end adjustments.

Account name	Debit £	Credit £

Task 11.13

When a trial balance was prepared, two ledger accounts were omitted:

Discounts received   £6,150

Discounts allowed   £7,500

To make the trial balance balance, a suspense account was opened.

What was the balance on the suspense account?

✓	
	Debit £1,350
	Credit £1,350
	Debit £13,650
	Credit £13,650

Task 11.14

The suspense account shows a debit balance of £100. This could be due to

✓	
	Entering £50 received from A Turner on the debit side of A Turner's account
	Entering £50 received from A Turner on the credit side of A Turner's account
	Undercasting the sales day book by £100
	Undercasting the sales ledger account by £100

Chapter 12

Task 12.1

A sole trader has balanced off his ledger accounts as at 31 May 20X8 and has now asked for your help in producing his financial statements.

(a) **Draw up and total the initial trial balance, inserting a balance for the suspense account as required.**

	£	Initial trial balance Debit £	Initial trial balance Credit £	Adjustments Debit £	Adjustments Credit £
Accumulated depreciation					
– furniture and fittings	6,100				
– motor vehicles	22,000				
Accrued expenses					
Allowance for doubtful debts	1,000				
Allowance for doubtful debts adjustment					
Bank overdraft	1,650				
Capital	74,000				
Depreciation expense – furniture & fittings					
Depreciation expense – motor vehicles					
Discounts allowed	2,100				
Discounts received	1,800				
Drawings	30,000				
Electricity	2,300				
Furniture and fittings at cost	24,500				
Insurance	3,000				

	Initial trial balance		Adjustments	
	£	Debit £	Credit £	Debit £	Credit £
Irrecoverable debts expense					
Miscellaneous expenses	1,200				
Motor expenses	3,400				
Motor vehicles at cost	48,000				
Prepayments					
Purchases	245,000				
Purchases ledger control	40,800				
Rent paid	4,200				
Sales	369,000				
Sales ledger control	61,500				
Inventory	41,000				
Suspense					
Telephone	1,600				
VAT due to HMRC	4,100				
Wages	52,000				

(b) A number of year end adjustments have yet to be made to the trial balance figures:

(i) Inventory at 31 May 20X8 has been valued at £43,500

(ii) The balances for accumulated depreciation are as at 1 June 20X7. Depreciation is to be provided at 30% on the reducing balance method on motor vehicles and at 10% straight line on the furniture and fittings

(iii) It has been decided that an irrecoverable debt of £1,500 should be written off and that the allowance for doubtful debts is to remain at 2% of remaining receivables

(iv) There are accruals of £650 of electricity and £350 of telephone

(v) Rent of £800 has already been paid for the quarter ended 31 August 20X8 and insurance includes £1,200 for the year ended 31 December 20X8

You are required to draft the journal entries required for these year end adjustments.

Account name	Debit £	Credit £

(c) Since the drafting of the initial trial balance a number of errors have come to light:

   (i) Motor expenses have been charged with £300 of miscellaneous expenses

   (ii) Discounts allowed of £425 and discounts received of £100 had been entered on the wrong side of the respective discounts accounts

You are required to draft the journal entries needed to correct these errors.

Account name	Debit £	Credit £

(d) **Put through the year end adjustments and the corrections of the errors in the adjustments column in (a) above and check that the two columns cast.**

Task 12.2

Given below is the list of balances for a business at its year end of 31 May 20X8.

	£
Inventory at 1 June 20X7	1,600
Motor vehicles at cost	23,800
Computer at cost	2,400
Furniture and fittings at cost	12,800
Accumulated depreciation at 1 June 20X7:	
Motor vehicles	12,140
Computer	600
Furniture and fittings	2,560
Wages	16,400
Telephone	900
Electricity	1,200
Advertising	400
Stationery	600
Motor expenses	1,700
Miscellaneous expenses	300
Insurance	1,000
Sales	86,400
Purchases	38,200
Sales ledger control account	7,200
Allowance for doubtful debts at 1 June 20X7	200
Bank (debit balance)	1,300
Petty cash	100
Purchases ledger control account	3,180
VAT (credit balance)	960
Capital	25,000
Drawings	21,140

You are also provided with the following information:

(i) The depreciation charge for the year has not yet been accounted for:

- Motor vehicles are to be depreciated at 30% on the reducing balance basis

- The computer is being depreciated at 25% on the straight-line basis

- The furniture and fittings are being depreciated at 20% on the straight-line basis

(ii) There is an accrual for electricity expenses of £400

(iii) There is £300 of prepaid insurance

(iv) The allowance for doubtful debts is to be 4% of the year end receivables

(v) £100 of advertising costs have been included in the stationery account

(vi) The closing inventory has been valued at £2,100.

You are required to:

(a) **enter the initial balances onto the extended trial balance given and check that the trial balance does balance**

(b) **enter each of the adjustments into the adjustments columns on the extended trial balance and total the adjustments columns**

(c) **extend the figures into the income statement and statement of financial position columns, and total the columns including calculating the profit and entering it into the statement of financial position columns**

Account name	Ledger balance		Adjustments		IS		SFP	
	Debit £	Credit £	Debit £	Credit £	Debit £	Credit £	Debit £	Credit £
Inventory at 1 June 20X7								
Motor vehicles at cost								
Computer at cost								
Furniture and fittings at cost								
Accumulated depreciation at 1 June 20X7:								
Motor vehicles								
Computer								
Furniture and fittings								
Wages								
Telephone								
Electricity								
Advertising								
Stationery								
Motor expenses								
Miscellaneous expenses								
Insurance								
Sales								
Purchases								
Sales ledger control								
Allowance for doubtful debts at 1 June 20X7								
Bank (debit balance)								
Petty cash								
Purchases ledger control								

Account name	Ledger balance		Adjustments		IS		SFP	
	Debit £	Credit £	Debit £	Credit £	Debit £	Credit £	Debit £	Credit £
VAT (credit balance)								
Capital								
Drawings								
Depreciation expense:								
Motor vehicles								
Computer								
Furniture and fittings								
Accruals								
Prepayments								
Allowance for doubtful debts adjustment								
Profit / loss								

Task 12.3

Given below is the list of balances for a business at the end of June 20X8.

	£
Capital	150,000
Purchases ledger control	40,400
Sales ledger control	114,500
Sales	687,000
Inventory at 1 July 20X7	40,400
Machinery at cost	68,000
Furniture and fittings at cost	32,400
Wages	98,700
Sales returns	4,800
Telephone	4,100
Purchases	485,000
Heat and light	3,400
Advertising	8,200
Purchases returns	3,000
Selling costs	9,400
Discounts received	4,700
Discounts allowed	3,900
Administrative expenses	14,800
Miscellaneous expense	400
Accumulated depreciation at 1 July 20X7:	
Plant and machinery	34,680
Furniture and fittings	6,480
Allowance for doubtful debts at 1 July 20X7	2,000
Drawings	36,860
Bank (debit balance)	6,400
VAT (credit balance)	3,200
Suspense account (debit balance)	200

You are also given the following information:

(a) The depreciation charges for the year are to be accounted for:

   (i) Depreciation on machinery is at the rate of 30% reducing balance

   (ii) Depreciation on furniture and fittings is at the rate of 20% straight line

(b) The suspense account balance has been investigated and the following errors have been discovered:

   (i) Discounts received of £450 had been posted to the purchases ledger control account but not to the discount account

   (ii) Sales returns of £480 were correctly posted to the sales ledger control account but were posted as £840 in the sales returns account

   (iii) A subtotal in the cash payments book of £1,010 for heat and light was not posted to the heat and light account

(c) An irrecoverable debt of £1,500 is to be written off and an allowance of 2% of receivables is required

(d) There is an accrual for telephone expenses of £400 and the administrative expenses include prepaid amounts of £700

(e) Closing inventory has been valued at £42,800

You are required to:

(a) **enter the ledger balances (including the suspense account) onto the extended trial balance given and total the trial balance to ensure that it agrees**

(b) **enter the adjustments in the adjustments columns and total them**

(c) **extend the extended trial balance into the income statement and statement of financial position columns, total the columns to find the profit or loss and extend this into the statement of financial position columns**

Account name	Ledger balance		Adjustments		IS		SFP	
	Debit £	Credit £	Debit £	Credit £	Debit £	Credit £	Debit £	Credit £
Capital								
Purchases ledger control								
Sales ledger control								
Sales								
Inventory at 1 June 20X7:								
Machinery at cost								
Furniture and fittings at cost								
Wages								
Sales returns								
Telephone								
Purchases								
Heat and light								
Advertising								
Purchases returns								
Selling costs								
Discount received								
Discount allowed								
Administrative expenses								
Miscellaneous expense								
Accumulated depreciation at 1 July 20X7								
Machinery								
Furniture and fittings								

Account name	Ledger balance		Adjustments		IS		SFP	
	Debit £	Credit £	Debit £	Credit £	Debit £	Credit £	Debit £	Credit £
Allowance for doubtful debts at 1 July 20X7								
Drawings								
Bank (debit balance)								
VAT (credit balance)								
Suspense account								
Depreciation expense:								
Machinery								
Furniture and fittings								
Allowance for doubtful debts adjustment								
Accruals								
Prepayments								
Profit / loss								

Task 12.4

Below is an alphabetical list of balances taken from the ledger of Clegg and Co, a sole trader, as at 31 May 20X8. You are also provided with some additional information.

	£
Administration costs	72,019.27
Bank overdraft	8,290.12
Capital	50,000.00
Loan	100,000.00
Depreciation charge	12,000.00
Drawings	36,000.00
Motor vehicles: cost	120,287.00
Motor vehicles: accumulated depreciation	36,209.28
Interest charges	12,182.26
Interest income	21.00
Wages	167,302.39
Purchases	104,293.38
Inventory as at 1 June 20X7	25,298.30
Purchases ledger control	42,190.85
Sales	481,182.20
Sales ledger control	156,293.00
VAT payable	4,938.20

(a) **Enter the balances in the format trial balance provided below. Set up a suspense account if necessary.**

(b) **With reference to the additional information below, clear the suspense account.**

(i) The debit side of the journal to record depreciation expense of £15,000.00 for the second six months of the period has been omitted.

(ii) An examination of administration costs shows that there is a prepayment for insurance of £320.00 and an accrual for electricity of £480.00.

(iii) One page of the sales returns day book was left out of the total posted to the sales ledger control account, although it was included in the other totals posted. The total value of credit notes on this page was £6,092.35.

(iv) Invoices totalling £6,283.38 have not been recorded in the purchases ledger accounts.

(v) The payment by BACS of wages in May of £14,248.40 has not been posted to the wages account, and nor has the purchase in May of a non-current asset for £4,000.00 been posted. This asset should be depreciated at a rate of 25% straight line, with a full year's depreciation being charged in the year of purchase.

(vi) A cash receipt of £10,000.00 was recorded in the cash book but, as it was not identified, it has not yet been posted. It has now been clarified that this represents additional capital from the owner.

(vii) Interest due of £650.00 on the loan needs to be accrued.

(viii) At 31 May 20X8 inventory on hand was valued at £32,125.28.

(c) **With reference to the additional information above, make whatever other adjustments to the trial balance are necessary.**

(d) (i) **Extend the trial balance**

(ii) **Total all columns of the extended trial balance.**

(iii) **Make entries to record the profit or loss for the year ended 31 May 20X8.**

Account name	Trial balance		Adjustments		IS		SFP	
	Debit £	Credit £	Debit £	Credit £	Debit £	Credit £	Debit £	Credit £
Administration costs								
Bank overdraft								
Capital								
Loan								
Depreciation charge								
Drawings								
Motor vehicles: Cost								
Motor vehicles: Depreciation								
Interest: paid								
Interest: received								
Wages								
Raw materials								
Inventory as at 1/6/X7								
Purchases ledger control								
Sales								
Sales ledger control								
Suspense								
VAT payable								
Accruals								
Prepayments								
Closing inventory								
Profit / loss								

Task 12.5

When an extended trial balance is extended and a business has made a profit, this figure for profit will be in the ⬚ debit/credit ⬚ column of the income statement.

Task 12.6

What is the double entry to record closing inventory on the ETB?

	Account name
Debit	
Credit	

Task 12.7

Which of these statements is/are correct?

(i)   A casting error in a day book will stop the trial balance balancing.

(ii) A transposition error in a daybook will stop the trial balance balancing.

✓	
	(i) only
	(i) and (ii)
	(ii) only
	Neither (i) or (ii)

Task 12.8

When a trial balance was prepared, two ledger accounts were omitted:

Discounts received   £2,050

Discounts allowed   £2,500

To make the trial balance balance a suspense account was opened.

What was the balance on the suspense account?

✓	
	Debit £450
	Credit £450
	Debit £4,550
	Credit £4,550

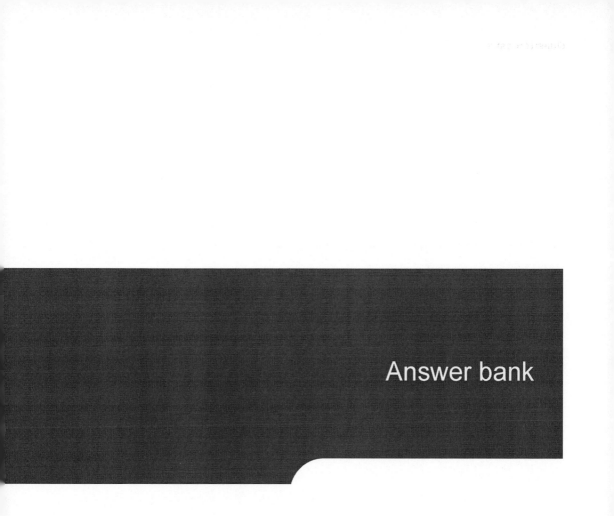

Answer bank

Answer bank

Accounts Preparation I Answer Bank

Chapter 1

Task 1.1

The sales returns day book lists	credit notes sent to customers
The purchases day book lists	invoices received from suppliers
The purchases returns day book lists	credit notes received from suppliers
The sales day book lists	invoices sent to customers

Task 1.2

What are the two effects of each of these transactions for accounting purposes?

Transaction	Account 1			Account 2		
	Name	Increase ✓	Decrease ✓	Name	Increase ✓	Decrease ✓
Payment of £15,000 into a business bank account by an individual in order to start up a business	bank	✓		capital	✓	
Payment by cheque of £2,000 for rent of a business property	bank		✓	rent expense	✓	
Payment by cheque of £6,200 for purchase of a delivery van	bank		✓	non-current asset	✓	
Payment by cheque of £150 for vehicle licence for the van	bank		✓	van expenses	✓	
Payment by cheque of £2,100 for goods for resale	bank		✓	purchases	✓	

Transaction	Account 1			Account 2		
	Name	Increase ✓	Decrease ✓	Name	Increase ✓	Decrease ✓
Sale of goods for cash and cheques of £870	bank	✓		sales	✓	
Purchase of goods for resale on credit for £2,800	purchases	✓		purchases ledger control	✓	
Payment by cheque for petrol of £80	bank		✓	van expenses	✓	
Sale of goods on credit for £3,400	sales	✓		sales ledger control	✓	
Payment by cheque of £1,500 to credit suppliers	bank		✓	purchases ledger control	✓	
Payment by cheque of electricity bill of £140	bank		✓	electricity expense	✓	
Receipt of cheque from credit customer of £1,600	bank	✓		sales ledger control	✓	
Withdrawal of £500 of cash for the owner's personal living costs	bank		✓	drawings	✓	
Payment by cheque for petrol of £70	bank		✓	van expenses	✓	

Task 1.3

Capital account

	£			£
		Bank		15,000

Bank account

	£		£
Capital	15,000	Rent	2,000
Sales	870	Van	6,200
Sales ledger control	1,600	Van expenses	150
		Purchases	2,100
		Van expenses	80
		Purchases ledger control	1,500
		Electricity	140
		Drawings	500
		Van expenses	70
		Balance c/d	4,730
			17,470
	17,470		
Balance b/d	4,730		

Rent account

	£		£
Bank	2,000		

Van account

	£		£
Bank	6,200		

Van expenses account

	£		£
Bank	150		
Bank	80		
Bank	70	Balance c/d	300
	300		300
Balance b/d	300		

Purchases account

	£		£
Bank	2,100		
Purchases ledger control	2,800	Balance c/d	4,900
	4,900		4,900
Balance b/d	4,900		

Sales account

	£		£
		Bank	870
Balance c/d	4,270	Sales ledger control	3,400
	4,270		4,270
		Balance b/d	4,270

Purchases ledger control account

	£		£
Bank	1,500	Purchases	2,800
Balance c/d	1,300		
	2,800		2,800
		Balance b/d	1,300

Sales ledger control account

	£		£
Sales	3,400	Bank	1,600
		Balance c/d	1,800
	3,400		3,400
Balance b/d	1,800		

Electricity account

	£		£
Bank	140		

Drawings account

	£		£
Bank	500		

Trial balance	Debit £	Credit £
Capital		15,000
Bank	4,730	
Rent	2,000	
Van	6,200	
Van expenses	300	
Purchases	4,900	
Sales		4,270
Payables ie purchases ledger control account		1,300
Receivables ie sales ledger control account	1,800	
Electricity	140	
Drawings	500	
	20,570	20,570

Task 1.4

✓	
	An asset or an expense
	A liability or an expense
	An amount owing to the organisation
✓	A liability or a revenue item

Chapter 2

Task 2.1

(a)

Concept	Materiality

(b)

Concept	Going concern

(c)

Concept	Accruals or matching

Task 2.2

Going concern and Accruals or matching

Task 2.3

	Non-current assets ✓	Current assets ✓	Liabilities ✓
A PC used in the accounts department of a retail store	✓		
A PC on sale in an office equipment shop		✓	
Wages due to be paid to staff at the end of the week			✓
A van for sale in a motor dealer's showroom		✓	
A delivery van used in a grocer's business	✓		
An amount owing to a bank for a loan for the acquisition of a van, to be repaid over 9 months			✓

Task 2.4

✓	
	On non-current assets, including repairs and maintenance
	On expensive assets
✓	Relating to the acquisition or improvement of non-current assets
	Incurred by the chief officer of the business

Improvements are capital expenditure, repairs and maintenance are not.

....

Chapter 3

Task 3.1

	Capital expenditure £	Revenue expenditure £
An SN63 sanding machine has been purchased at a cost of £12,000 plus VAT. The delivery charge was £400. After its initial run it was cleaned at a cost of £100.	12,400	100
A building has been purchased at a cost of £120,000. The surveyor's fees were an additional £400 and the legal fees £1,200. The building has been re-decorated at a total cost of £13,000.	121,600	13,000
A new main server has been purchased at a cost of £10,600. In order to house the server a room in the building has had to have a special air conditioning unit fitted at a cost of £2,450. The server's cost includes software worth £1,000 and CDs with a value of £100.	12,950	100
A salesperson's car has been purchased at a cost of £14,000 plus VAT. The invoice also shows delivery costs of £50 (inclusive of VAT) and road fund licence of £160 (no VAT charged). The car is available for private use by the salesperson.	16,850	160

Notes

(1) The computer software could be treated as either capital or revenue expenditure. As the cost is quite large it would probably be treated as capital expenditure. The total capital expenditure is therefore 10,600 – 100 + 2,450 = 12,950.

(2) VAT is irrecoverable on both the purchase price of cars and delivery charges for cars. The amount of expenditure which is capitalised is therefore the VAT inclusive purchase price of the car (£14,000 × 1.20 = £16,800) plus the delivery charges (£50 including VAT).

··

Task 3.2

The SPK100 repairs would be treated as

	capital expenditure
✓	revenue expenditure

The FL11 repairs would be treated as

✓	
✓	capital expenditure
	revenue expenditure

....

Task 3.3

(a)

	Debit £	Credit £
Motor vehicles account (12,000 + (12,000 × 20%))	14,400	
Motor expenses account	150	
Bank account		14,550

(b)

	Debit £	Credit £
Machinery account (15,400 + 1,400)	16,800	
VAT account (15,400 × 0.20)	3,080	
Purchases ledger control account (15,400 + 3,080)		18,480
Wages account		1,400

(c)

	Debit £	Credit £
Computer account (3,800 – 150)	3,650	
Computer expenses account	150	
VAT account (3,800 × 20%)	760	
Bank account (3,800 + 760)		4,560

(d)

	Debit £	Credit £
Building maintenance account	800	
Bank account		800

(e)

	Debit £	Credit £
Computer expenses account	200	
Bank account		200

Task 3.4

Machinery account

	£		£
Balance b/d	103,400.00		
Bank	13,500.00		
Wages	400.00		
Purchases	850.00		

Buildings account

	£		£
Balance b/d	200,000.00		
Bank (150,000 + 20,000)	170,000.00		

VAT account

	£		£
Bank: VAT on machinery (13,500 × 20%)	2,700.00	Balance b/d	13,289.60

Purchases account

	£		£
Balance b/d	56,789.50	Machinery	850.00

BPP
LEARNING MEDIA

Wages account

	£		£
Balance b/d	113,265.88	Machinery	400.00

Buildings maintenance account

	£		£
Balance b/d	10,357.00		
Bank	4,000.00		

Bank account

	£		£
Balance b/d	214,193.60	Machinery & VAT	
		(13,500 + 2,700)	16,200.00
		Buildings	170,000.00
		Buildings maintenance	4,000.00

Task 3.5

✓	
✓	True
	False

Task 3.6

Which of the following costs would be classified as capital expenditure for a restaurant business?

✓	
	A replacement for a broken window
	Repainting the restaurant
✓	An illuminated sign advertising the business name
	Knives and forks for the restaurant

Replacing a broken window is a repair, so it is revenue expenditure. Repainting the restaurant is a repair and renewal expense so this too is revenue. Knives and forks are not likely to be expensive enough to be treated as capital expenditure.

Chapter 4

Task 4.1

Accruals or matching

Task 4.2

	Workings	Depreciation charge £	Carrying amount £
Machine purchased for £17,400 on 1 January 20X6 with a useful life of 5 years and a zero residual value.	£17,400/5 years £17,400 – (3 × 3,480)	3,480	 6,960
Machine purchased for £12,800 on 1 January 20X7 with a useful life of 4 years and a residual value of £2,000.	$\dfrac{12,800 - 2,000}{4\,\text{years}}$ £12,800 – (2 × 2,700)	2,700	 7,400
Computer purchased for £4,600 on 1 January 20X8 with a useful life of 3 years and an estimated resale value of £700.	$\dfrac{4,600 - 700}{3\,\text{years}}$ £4,600 – 1,300	1,300	 3,300

Task 4.3

	Workings	Depreciation charge £	Carrying amount £
Machinery costing £24,600 purchased on 1 April 20X8 which is to be depreciated at 20% on the reducing balance basis.	£24,600 × 20% £24,600 – £4,920	4,920	19,680
Motor vehicle costing £18,700 purchased on 1 April 20X6 which is to be depreciated at 20% on the reducing balance basis.	Y/e 31/3/X7: 18,700 × 20% = 3,740 18,700 – 3,740 = 14,960 Y/e 31/3/X8: 14,960 × 20% = 2,992 14,960 – 2,992 = 11,968 Y/e 31/3/X9: 11,968 x 20% = 2,394 11,968 – 2,394 = 9,574	2,394	9,574
Computer costing £3,800 purchased on 1 April 20X7 which is to be depreciated at 30% on the reducing balance basis.	Y/e 31/3/X8: 3,800 × 30% = 1,140 3,800 – 1,140 = 2,660 Y/e 31/3/X9: 2,660 x 30% = 798 2,660 – 798 = 1,862	798	1,862

Task 4.4

	Workings	Depreciation charge £
Machine purchased on 1 May 20X8 for £14,000. This is to be depreciated at the rate of 20% per annum on the straight-line basis.	£14,000 × 20% × 8/12	1,866.67
Office furniture and fittings purchased on 1 June 20X8 for £3,200. These are to be depreciated on the reducing balance basis at a rate of 25% with a full year's charge in the year of purchase and no charge in the year of disposal.	£3,200 × 25%	800.00
Computer purchased on 31 October 20X8 for £4,400. This is to be depreciated at the rate of 40% per annum on the straight-line basis.	£4,400 × 40% × 2/12	293.33

Task 4.5

	Workings	Depreciation charge £
20X0	1,800 × 60%	1,080
20X1	(1,800 – 1,080) × 60%	432
20X2	(1,800 – 1,080 – 432) × 60%	173
20X3	(1,800 – 1,080 – 432 – 173) × 60%	69

Task 4.6

Debit	Depreciation charge account
Credit	Accumulated depreciation account

Task 4.7

	£605
✓	£363
	£179
	£72

Workings

	£
Cost	2,800
Depreciation to 31 Dec X4 (2,800 × 40%)	1,120
Carrying amount at 31 Dec X4	1,680
Depreciation to 31 Dec X5 (1,680 × 40%)	672
Carrying amount at 31 Dec X5	1,008
Depreciation to 31 Dec X6 (1,008 × 40%)	403
Carrying amount at 31 Dec X6	605
Depreciation to 31 Dec X7 (605 × 40%)	242
Carrying amount at 31 Dec X7	363

Task 4.8

✓	To allocate the cost less residual value of a non-current asset over the accounting periods expected to benefit from its use
	To ensure that funds are available for the eventual replacement of the asset
	To reduce the cost of the asset to its estimated market value
	To recognise the fact that assets lose their value over time

Chapter 5

Task 5.1

loss	of £	125

Workings

		£
1 Apr 20X7	Cost	12,500
31 Mar 20X8	Depreciation	(3,750)
Carrying amount		8,750
31 Mar 20X9	Depreciation	(2,625)
Carrying amount		6,125
Proceeds		(6,000)
Loss on disposal		125

Task 5.2

Workings

$$\text{Annual depreciation charge} = \frac{£25,000 - 3,000}{5}$$

$$= £4,400$$

Non-current asset at cost account

	£		£
1 Jan 20X6 Bank	25,000	31 Dec 20X8 Disposal	25,000

Depreciation account

	£		£
31 Dec 20X6 Accumulated depreciation	4,400	31 Dec 20X6 Income statement	4,400
31 Dec 20X7 Accumulated depreciation	4,400	31 Dec 20X7 Income statement	4,400
31 Dec 20X8 Accumulated depreciation	4,400	31 Dec 20X8 Income statement	4,400

Accumulated depreciation account

	£		£
31 Dec 20X7 Balance c/d	8,800	31 Dec 20X6 Expense	4,400
		31 Dec 20X7 Expense	4,400
	8,800		8,800
31 Dec 20X8 Disposal	13,200	1 Jan 20X8 Balance b/d	8,800
		31 Dec 20X8 Expense	4,400
	13,200		13,200

Disposal account

	£		£
31 Dec 20X8 Cost	25,000	31 Dec 20X8 Accumulated depreciation	13,200
		31 Dec 20X8 Bank	11,000
		31 Dec 20X8 Income statement	800
	25,000		25,000

··

Task 5.3

		£
1 Apr 20X7	Cost	13,800
31 Mar 20X8	Depreciation	(4,140)
Carrying amount		9,660
31 Mar 20X9	Depreciation	(2,898)
Carrying amount		6,762

Depreciation expense account

	£		£
31 Mar 20X9 Acc dep	2,898		

Accumulated depreciation account

	£		£
31 Mar 20X9 Disposal	7,038	1 Apr 20X8 Balance b/d	4,140
		31 Mar 20X9 Expense	2,898
	7,038		7,038

Motor vehicle at cost account

	£		£
1 Apr 20X8 Balance b/d	13,800	31 Mar 20X9 Disposal	13,800

Disposal account

	£		£
31 Mar 20X9 Cost	13,800	31 Mar 20X9 Acc dep	7,038
31 Mar 20X9 Profit	238	31 Mar 20X9 Bank	7,000
	14,038		14,038

Task 5.4

Disposal account

	£		£
30 Nov 20X8 Cost	15,600	30 Nov 20X8 Acc dep	9,425
		30 Nov 20X8 Bank	6,000
		30 Nov 20X8 Loss – IS	175
	15,600		15,600

Workings

Depreciation at the date of disposal:

		£
31 December 20X6	15,600 × 25% × 6/12	1,950
31 December 20X7	15,600 × 25%	3,900
31 December 20X8	15,600 × 25% × 11/12	3,575
		9,425

Task 5.5

✓	
	Profit of £600
	Loss of £600
	Profit of £350
✓	Loss of £400

Workings

(£5,000 cost – £1,000 residual value) / 4 = £1,000 depreciation per annum. Carrying amount on disposal was therefore £2,000.

Chapter 6

Task 6.1

Telephone account

	£		£
31 Mar Bank	845	31 Mar Income statement	1,015
31 Mar Balance c/d	170		
	1,015		1,015

Task 6.2

Electricity account

	£		£
30 June Bank	2,300	30 June Income statement	3,200
30 June Balance c/d	900		
	3,200		3,200

Task 6.3

Insurance account

	£		£
31 May Bank	2,300	31 May Balance c/d	250
		31 May Income statement	2,050
	2,300		2,300

Task 6.4

Rent account

	£		£
30 June Bank	4,500	30 June Balance c/d	400
		30 June Income statement	4,100
	4,500		4,500

Task 6.5

Rental income account

	£		£
30 June Income in advance	350	30 June Bank	5,600
c/d	5,250		
30 June Income statement	5,600		5,600
	350		

Task 6.6

✓	
	Overstated by £375
	Overstated by £750
	Understated by £375
✓	Understated by £750

An accrual of £375 should have been set up, which would have increased the electricity expense for the year by £375. Instead a prepayment was set up, decreasing the expense by £375. Setting up the prepayment instead of an accrual has therefore understated the expense for the year by £750 (2 × £375).

Task 6.7

£	18,388.23

	£
Paid in year	14,060.55
Accrual (2/3 × £6,491.52)	4,327.68
	18,388.23

Task 6.8

£	900

Workings

Rent payable

20X1		£	20X1		£
31 Dec	Bank	1,275	1 Jan	Balance b/d	250
			31 Dec	Balance c/d (1/3 × £375)	125
				Income statement	900
		1,275			1,275

....

Task 6.9

✓	
	£4,000
✓	£4,500
	£5,000
	£5,500

Working

Rental income account

	£		£
Balance b/d	1,000	Bank	5,000
Income statement	4,500	Balance c/d	500
	5,500		5,500

....

Chapter 7

Task 7.1

£	25.10 (£24.60 + £0.5)

Net realisable value

£	24.80 (£25.80 – £1)

Value in the extended trial balance

£	3,100 (125 × £24.80)

Task 7.2

Inventory line	Quantity – units	Cost £	Selling price £	Selling costs £	Value per unit £	Total value £
A	180	12.50	20.40	0.50	12.50	2,250
B	240	10.90	12.60	1.80	10.80	2,592
C	300	15.40	22.70	1.20	15.40	4,620
D	80	16.50	17.80	1.50	16.30	1,304
E	130	10.60	18.00	1.00	10.60	1,378
						12,144

Task 7.3

		£
(a)	the FIFO method	435
(b)	the AVCO method	432

Workings

(a) FIFO

Opening balance		80 units @ 8.20
Purchases		100 units @ 8.50
Sales	80 units @ 8.20	
	60 units @ 8.50	
	140 units	
	80 units @ 8.20	
Purchases		180 units @ 8.70
Sales	40 units @ 8.50	
	60 units @ 8.70	
	100 units	
Sales	70 units @ 8.70	
Closing inventory	50 units @ 8.70	£435.00

(b) AVCO

	Average cost	Quantity	Value £
Opening balance	8.20	80	656
Purchases	8.50	100	850
	8.37	180	1,506
Sales	8.37	(140)	(1,172)
		40	334
Sales	8.70	180	1,566
	8.64	220	1,900
Sales	8.64	(100)	(864)
Sales	8.64	(70)	(604)
	8.64	50	432

···

Task 7.4

> **The lower of cost and net realisable value**

···

Task 7.5

£	10,405

Workings

The settlement discount is irrelevant here.

	Cost less 2½% trade discount £	NRV £	Valuation £
Product A	3,510.00	5,100.00	3,510.00
Product B	2,827.50	2,800.00	2,800.00
Product C	4,095.00	4,100.00	4,095.00
			10,405.00

Task 7.6

✓	
	The expected selling price of the inventory
✓	The expected selling price less disposal costs
	The replacement cost of the inventory
	The market price

Net realisable value is the amount that can be obtained, less any further expenses incurred to bring the inventory to a condition in which it can be sold.

Chapter 8

Task 8.1

General ledger

Sales ledger control account

	£		£
Balance b/d	5,479	Irrecoverable debts expense (321 + 124)	445
		Balance c/d	5,034
	5,479		5,479
Balance b/d	5,034		

Irrecoverable debts expense account

	£		£
Sales ledger control	445	Income statement	445

Sales ledger

G Simms & Co

	£		£
Balance b/d	321	Irrecoverable debts	321

L Fitzgerald

	£		£
Balance b/d	124	Irrecoverable debts	124

··

Task 8.2

General ledger

Sales ledger control account

	£		£
30 Sep Balance b/d	16,475	30 Sep Irrecoverable debts expense (1,200 + 470)	1,670
		30 Sep Balance c/d	14,805
	16,475		16,475

Irrecoverable debts expense account

	£			£
30 Sep Sales ledger control	1,670	30 Sep Income statement		1,670

Sales ledger

H Maguire

	£			£
30 Sep Balance b/d	1,200	30 Sep Irrecoverable debts		1,200

J Palmer

	£			£
30 Sep Balance b/d	470	30 Sep Irrecoverable debts		470

Task 8.3

General ledger

Sales ledger control account

		£			£
31 Dec 20X8	Balance b/d	7,264	31 Dec 20X8	Irrecoverable debts expense	669
			31 Dec 20X8	Balance c/d	6,595
		7,264			7,264

Irrecoverable debts expense account

		£			£
31 Dec 20X8	Sales ledger control	669	31 Dec 20X8	Bank	488
			31 Dec 20X8	Income statement	181
		669			669

Sales ledger

R Trevor

	£		£

E Ingham

	£		£
31 Dec 2008 Balance b/d	669	31 Dec 2008 Irrecoverable debts	669

Task 8.4

Sales ledger control account

	£		£
Balance b/d	218,940	Irrecoverable debt expense	2,440
		Balance c/d	216,500
	218,940		218,940

Allowance for doubtful debts account

	£		£
		Balance b/d	5,215
Balance c/d (£216,500 x 3%)	6,495	Allowance for doubtful debts adjustment	1,280
	6,495		6,495

Irrecoverable debts expense account

	£		£
Sales ledger control account	2,440	Income statement	2,440

Allowance for doubtful debts adjustment account

	£		£
Allowance for doubtful debts	1,280	Income statement	1,280

Task 8.5

✓	
	Accruals
	Consistency
	Materiality
✓	Prudence

Chapter 9

Task 9.1

(a)

Account name	Amount £	Debit (✓)	Credit (✓)
Purchases ledger control account	20	✓	
Bank	20		✓

(b) Bank interest received on the bank statement of £45.

Account name	Amount £	Debit (✓)	Credit (✓)
Bank	45	✓	
Interest received	45		✓

(c) A BACs receipt from a customer for £5,400 has not been entered in the cash

Account name	Amount £	Debit (✓)	Credit (✓)
Bank	5,400	✓	
Sales ledger control account	5,400		✓

(d) Cheque number 10810 for £2,356 issued on 29 May, in respect of payment of an invoice for accountancy services, is not showing on the bank statement.

Note for bank reconciliation:

The cheque should appear as an unpresented cheque in the bank reconciliation. It should be deducted from the balance per the bank statement.

Task 9.2

Adjustment	Amount £	Debit ✓	Credit ✓
1. Bank charges	25	✓	
Bank	25		✓
3. Sales ledger control (£895 - £859)	36		✓
Bank	36	✓	

Notes: For point 2, it is the bank statement that must be corrected, not the cash book. Point 4 relates to an uncredited lodgement which will appear on the bank reconciliation statement.

••

Task 9.3

Bank reconciliation as at 7 July

	£
Balance per bank statement at 7 July	12,848.66
Add: Outstanding lodgements	
S Rose	485.21
W Field Suppliers	720.15
R Forge	225.63
Total to add	1,430.99
Less: Unpresented cheques	
003124 (still unpaid from previous reconciliation)	589.45
003126	126.89
003127	500.00
003128	896.78
003129	663.14
003130	105.45
003131	4,325.00
Total to subtract:	7,206.71
Balance as per cash book (5,982.91 + 16,372.85 – 15,282.82)	7,072.94

Task 9.4

✓	
	Timing difference
	Bank charges
	Error
✓	Cash receipts total posted to purchases ledger control account

The incorrect posting of the total will not affect the bank reconciliation.

Chapter 10

Task 10.1

Sales ledger control account

	£		£
Balance b/d	4,268	Sales returns	995
Credit sales	15,487	Irrecoverable debt written off	210
Returned cheque	645	Cheques from customers	13,486
		Discounts allowed	408
		Contra	150
		Balance c/d	5,151
	20,400		20,400

Task 10.2

Purchases ledger control account

	£		£
Cheques to suppliers	10,379	Balance b/d	3,299
Returns to suppliers	1,074	Credit purchases	12,376
Discounts received	302		
Contra	230		
Balance c/d	3,690		
	15,675		15,675

Task 10.3

Sales ledger control account

	£		£
Balance b/d	12,634	Cheques from customers	50,375
Credit sales	51,376	Sales returns	3,173
		Contra	630
		Discounts allowed	1,569
		Balance c/d	8,263
	64,010		64,010

Purchases ledger control account

	£		£
Discounts received	1,245	Balance b/d	10,553
Cheques to suppliers	35,795	Credit purchases	40,375
Purchases returns	2,003		
Contra	630		
Balance c/d	11,255		
	50,928		50,928

Task 10.4

Adjustment	Amount £	Debit ✓	Credit ✓
Adjustment for (a)	1,000	✓	
Adjustment for (b)	90	✓	

Task 10.5

Adjustment	Amount £	Debit ✓	Credit ✓
Adjustment for (a)	576	✓	
Adjustment for (b)	169	✓	
Adjustment for (d)	100		✓

Task 10.6

Account name	Debit	Credit
	£	£
Sales (1,440.00 × 5/6)	1,200.00	
VAT (1,440.00 × 1/6)	240.00	
Sales ledger control		1,440.00
Purchases ledger control	582.45	
Sales ledger control		582.45
Purchases ledger control		900.00
Sales	900.00	
Being correction of errors in sales ledger control account		
Marketing (872.00 × 5/6)	726.67	
VAT (872.00 × 1/6)	145.33	
Purchases ledger control		872.00
Purchases ledger control		270.00
Despatch	270.00	
Being correction of errors in purchases ledger control account		

....

Task 10.7

✓	
✓	The sales day book has been undercast by £1,000
	Settlement discounts totalling £1,000 have been omitted from the general ledger
	One sales ledger account with a credit balance of £1,000 has been treated as a debit balance
	The cash receipts book has been undercast by £1,000

Explanation

The total of sales invoices in the day book is debited to the control account. If the total is understated by £1,000, the debits in the control account will also be understated by £1,000. Options B and D would have the opposite effect: credit entries in the control account would be understated. Option C would lead to a discrepancy of 2 × £1,000 = £2,000.

Task 10.8

✓	Control account	List of balances
	Debit £45	Add £45
✓	Credit £45	Add £45
	Debit £45	Subtract £45
	Credit £45	Subtract £45

Explanation

This affects both the total which was posted to the control account and the individual posting to the purchases ledger.

Task 10.9

✓	Control account	List of balances
	Debit purchases ledger control	Credit sales ledger control
	Credit purchases ledger control	Credit sales ledger control
	Debit sales ledger control	Credit purchases ledger control
✓	Credit sales ledger control	Debit purchases ledger control

Both the amount due from customers and the amount due to suppliers are being reduced by discounts allowed and discounts received respectively.

Chapter 11

Task 11.1

Error	Imbalance ✓	No imbalance ✓
The payment of the telephone bill was posted to the cash payments book and then credited to the telephone account	✓	
The depreciation expense was debited to the accumulated depreciation account and credited to the depreciation expense account		✓
The electricity account balance of £750 was taken to the trial balance as £570	✓	
The motor expenses were debited to the motor vehicles at cost account		✓
The discounts received in the cash payments book were not posted to the general ledger		✓

Task 11.2

£	8,304	Credit balance

Task 11.3

(a)

Account name	Debit £	Credit £
Telephone account	236	
Electricity account		236
Being correction of misposting of telephone expense		

(b)

Account name	Debit £	Credit £
Sales ledger control account	180	
Sales account		180
Being correction of sales invoice entry in the sales day book		

(c)

Account name	Debit £	Credit £
Purchases ledger control account	38	
Purchases returns account		38
Being entry of credit note omitted from purchases returns day book		

(d)

Account name	Debit £	Credit £
Allowance for doubtful debts adjustment account	254	
Allowance for doubtful debts		254
Being correction of error in increasing allowance for doubtful debts		

(e)

Account name	Debit £	Credit £
Purchases ledger control account	400	
Sales ledger control account		400
Being correction of misposting of contra entry		

Task 11.4

Suspense account

	£		£
Sales ledger control	2,700	Balance b/d	1,370
Sales ledger control (£235 × 2)	470	Wages – trial balance	1,800
	3,170		3,170

Task 11.5

Suspense account

	£		£
Balance b/d	3,100	Insurance (1,585 × 2)	3,170
Postage (62 – 26)	36		
Bank interest received – TB	34		
	3,170		3,170

Task 11.6

Account name	Debit £	Credit £
Accumulated depreciation	10,500	
Disposal account	15,000	
Suspense	4,000	
Non-current asset at cost		15,000
Disposal account		10,500
Disposal account		4,000

Task 11.7

Account name	Debit £	Credit £
Suspense	1,641.38	
Wages		270.00
Purchases ledger control		180.00
Sales ledger control		1,191.38

Task 11.8

transposition error
error of omission
error of commission
error of principle
reversal of entries

Note: Other examples of errors as set out in Chapter 11 are also acceptable

Task 11.9

The total of debit balances in the TB therefore | exceeds | the total of credit balances by

£	500

Task 11.10

✓			
	Debit	Discounts received	£350
	Credit	Suspense	£350
	Debit	Suspense	£350
	Credit	Discounts received	£350
	Debit	Discounts received	£700
	Credit	Suspense	£700
✓	Debit	Suspense	£700
	Credit	Discounts received	£700

Task 11.11

	Workings	£
Rent	£3,600 + £1,200	4,800
Insurance	£4,250 − £850	3,400

Task 11.12

Account name		Debit £	Credit £
(i)	Selling expenses	340	
	Bank		340
(ii)	Purchases	360	
	Suspense		360
(iii)	Suspense	690	
	Discount received		690
(iv)	Inventory – SFP	18,200	
	Inventory – income statement		18,200
(v)	Irrecoverable debts expense	2,800	
	Sales ledger control		2,800
	Allowance for doubtful debts		
	(£20,200 – 2,800) × 2% – 300	48	
	Irrecoverable debts expense		48
(vi)	Administration expenses	680	
	Accrued expenses		680
	Being accrued administration expenses		
(vii)	Prepayments of expenses	440	
	Administration expenses		440
(viii)	Depreciation expense – machinery (£58,400 × 20%)	11,680	
	Accumulated depreciation – machinery		11,680
	Depreciation expense – motor vehicles (£22,100 – 9,680) × 25%	3,105	
	Accumulated depreciation – motor vehicles		3,105
	Purchases	340	

Task 11.13

✓	
✓	Debit £1,350
	Credit £1,350
	Debit £13,650
	Credit £13,650

Task 11.14

The suspense account shows a debit balance of £100. This could be due to

✓	
	Entering £50 received from A Turner on the debit side of A Turner's account
	Entering £50 received from A Turner on the credit side of A Turner's account
	Undercasting the sales day book by £100
✓	Undercasting the sales ledger account by £100

The first two options will affect only the personal ledger account of A Turner. The third option will affect both sides of the double entry.

Chapter 12

Task 12.1

(a)

	£	Initial trial balance		Adjustments	
	£	Debit £	Credit £	Debit £	Credit £
Accumulated depreciation					
– furniture and fittings	6,100		6,100		2,450
– motor vehicles	22,000		22,000		7,800
Accrued expenses					1,000
Allowance for doubtful debts	1,000		1,000		200
Allowance for doubtful debts adjustment				200	
Bank overdraft	1,650		1,650		
Capital	74,000		74,000		
Depreciation expense – furniture & fittings				2,450	
Depreciation expense – motor vehicles				7,800	
Discounts allowed	2,100	2,100		850	
Discounts received	1,800		1,800		200
Drawings	30,000	30,000			
Electricity	2,300	2,300		650	
Furniture and fittings at cost	24,500	24,500			
Insurance	3,000	3,000			700
Irrecoverable debts expense				1,500	
Miscellaneous expenses	1,200	1,200		300	
Motor expenses	3,400	3,400			300
Motor vehicles at cost	48,000	48,000			
Prepayments				1,500	

	£	Initial trial balance		Adjustments	
		Debit £	Credit £	Debit £	Credit £
Purchases	245,000	245,000			
Purchases ledger control	40,800		40,800		
Rent paid	4,200	4,200			800
Sales	369,000		369,000		
Sales ledger control	61,500	61,500			1,500
Inventory	41,000	41,000		43,500	43,500
Suspense		650		200	850
Telephone	1,600	1,600		350	
VAT due to HMRC	4,100		4,100		
Wages	52,000	52,000			
		520,450	520,450	59,300	59,300

(b)

Account name	Debit £	Credit £
Inventory – statement of financial position	43,500	
Inventory – income statement		43,500
Depreciation expense – furniture and fittings (£24,500 × 10%)	2,450	
Accumulated depreciation – furniture and fittings		2,450
Depreciation expense – motor vehicles ((£48,000 – £22,000) × 30%)	7,800	
Accumulated depreciation – motor vehicles		7,800
Irrecoverable debts expense	1,500	
Sales ledger control account		1,500
Allowance for doubtful debts adjustment (((£61,500 – £1,500) × 2%) – £1,000)	200	
Allowance for doubtful debts		200
Electricity	650	

Account name	Debit £	Credit £
Telephone	350	
Accrued expenses		1,000
Prepayments	1,500	
Rent		800
Insurance (£1,200 × 7/12)		700

(c)

Account name	Debit £	Credit £
Miscellaneous expenses	300	
Motor expenses		300
Discounts allowed (£425 x 2)	850	
Suspense		850
Suspense	200	
Discounts received (£100 x 2)		200

Task 12.2

Workings

Depreciation on motor vehicles: £(23,800 − 12,140) × 30% = £3,498

Depreciation on computer: £2,400 × 25% = £600

Depreciation on furniture and fittings: £12,800 × 20% = £2,560

Account name	Ledger balance Debit £	Ledger balance Credit £	Adjustments Debit £	Adjustments Credit £	IS Debit £	IS Credit £	SFP Debit £	SFP Credit £
Inventory at 1 June 20X7	1,600		2,100	2,100	1,600	2,100	2,100	
Motor vehicles at cost	23,800						23,800	
Computer at cost	2,400						2,400	
Furniture and fittings at cost	12,800						12,800	
Accumulated depreciation at 1 June 20X7:								
Motor vehicles		12,140		3,498				15,638
Computer		600		600				1,200
Furniture and fittings		2,560		2,560				5,120
Wages	16,400				16,400			
Telephone	900				900			
Electricity	1,200		400		1,600			
Advertising	400		100		500			
Stationery	600			100	500			
Motor expenses	1,700				1,700			
Miscellaneous expenses	300				300			
Insurance	1,000			300	700			
Sales		86,400				86,400		
Purchases	38,200				38,200			
Sales ledger control	7,200						7,200	
Allowance for doubtful debts at 1 June 20X7		200		88				288
Bank (debit balance)	1,300						1,300	
Petty cash	100						100	
Purchases ledger control		3,180						3,180

Account name	Ledger balance		Adjustments		IS		SFP	
	Debit £	Credit £	Debit £	Credit £	Debit £	Credit £	Debit £	Credit £
VAT (credit balance)		940						960
Capital		25,000						25,000
Drawings	21,140						21,140	
Depreciation expense:								
Motor vehicles			3,498		3,498			
Computer			600		600			
Furniture and fittings			2,560		2,560			
Accruals				400				400
Prepayments			300				300	
Allowance for doubtful debts adjustment			88		88			
Profit / loss					19,354			19,354
	131,040	131,040	9,646	9,646	88,500	88,500	71,140	71,140

Task 12.3

Workings

Depreciation on machinery: £(68,000 – 34,680) × 30% = £9,996
Depreciation on furniture and fittings: £32,400 × 20% = £6,480

Ledger account	Ledger balances		Adjustments		Income statement		Statement of financial position	
	Dr £	Cr £	Dr £	Cr £	Dr £	Cr £	Dr £	Cr £
Capital		150,000						150,000
Purchases ledger control		40,400						40,400
Sales ledger control	114,500			1,500			113,000	
Sales		687,000				687,000		
Inventory at 1 July 20X7	40,400		42,800	42,800	40,400	42,800	42,800	
Machinery at cost	68,000						68,000	
Furniture and fittings at cost	32,400						32,400	
Wages	98,700				98,700			
Sales returns	4,800			360	4,440			
Telephone	4,100		400		4,500			
Purchases	485,000				485,000			
Heat and light	3,400		1,010		4,410			
Advertising	8,200				8,200			
Purchases returns		3,000				3,000		
Selling costs	9,400				9,400			
Discounts received		4,700		450		5,150		
Discounts allowed	3,900				3,900			
Administrative expenses	14,800			700	14,100			
Miscellaneous expenses	400				400			
Accumulated depreciation at 1 July 20X7:								
Machinery		34,680		9,996				44,676
Furniture and fittings		6,480		6,480				12,960
Allowance for doubtful debts at 1 July 20X7		2,000		260				2,260

Ledger account	Ledger balances		Adjustments		Income statement		Statement of financial position	
	Dr £	Cr £	Dr £	Cr £	Dr £	Cr £	Dr £	Cr £
Drawings	36,860						36,860	
Bank (debit balance)	6,400						6,400	
VAT (credit balance)		3,200						3,200
Suspense account (debit balance)	200		450 360	1,010				
Depreciation expenses:								
Machinery			9,996		9,996			
Furniture and fittings			6,480		6,480			
Irrecoverable debt expense			1,500		1,500			
Allowance for doubtful debts adjustment			260		260			
Accruals				400				400
Prepayments			700				700	
Profit					46,264			46,264
	931,460	931,460	63,956	63,956	737,950	737,950	300,160	300,160

Task 12.4

Account name	Trial balance		Adjustments		IS		SFP	
	Debit £	Credit £	Debit £	Credit £	Debit £	Credit £	Debit £	Credit £
Administration costs	72,019.27		480.00	320.00	72,179.27			
Bank overdraft		8,290.12						8,290.12
Capital		50,000.00		10,000.00				60,000.00
Loan		100,000.00						100,000.00
Depreciation charge	12,000.00		16,000.00		28,000.00			
Drawings	36,000.00		4,000.00				36,000.00	
Non-current assets: Cost	120,287.00						124,287.00	
Non-current assets: Depreciation		36,209.28		1,000.00				37,209.28
Interest: paid	12,182.26		650.00		12,832.26			
Interest: received		21.00				21.00		
Wages	167,302.39		14,248.40		181,550.79			
Raw materials	104,293.38				104,293.38			
Inventory as at 1/6/X7	25,298.30				25,298.30			
Purchases ledger control		42,190.85						42,190.85
Sales		481,182.20				481,182.20		
Sales ledger control	156,293.00			6,092.35			150,200.65	
Suspense	17,156.05		6,092.35	15,000.00				
			10,000.00	14,248.40				
				4,000.00				
VAT payable		4,938.20		480.00				4,938.20
Accruals				650.00				1,130.00
Prepayments			320.00				320.00	
Closing inventory			32,125.28	32,125.28		32,125.28	32,125.28	
Profit					89,174.48			89,174.48
	722,831.65	722,831.65	83,916.03	83,916.03	513,328.48	513,328.48	342,932.93	342,932.93

Task 12.5

When an extended trial balance is extended and a business has made a profit, this figure for profit will be in the [debit] column of the income statement.

··

Task 12.6

What is the double entry to record closing inventory on the ETB?

	Account name
Debit	Inventory – statement of financial position
Credit	Inventory – income statement

··

Task 12.7

Which of these statements is/are correct?

(i)   A casting error in a day book will stop the trial balance balancing.

(ii) A transposition error in a daybook will stop the trial balance balancing.

✓	
	(i) only
	(i) and (ii)
	(ii) only
✓	Neither (i) or (ii)

··

Task 12.8

✓	
✓	Debit £450
	Credit £450
	Debit £4,550
	Credit £4,550

Working

Suspense account

	£		£
Balance b/d	450		
Discounts received	2,050	Discounts allowed	2,500
	2,500		2,500

Answer bank

AAT PRACTICE ASSESSMENT 1
ACCOUNTS PREPARATION I

Time allowed: 2 hours

Section 1

Task 1.1

This task is about recording information for non-current assets for a business known as AMBR Trading. AMBR Trading is registered for VAT and has a financial year end of 31 March.

The following is a purchase invoice received by AMBR Trading relating to some items to be used in its warehouse:

To: AMBR Trading Unit 6, East End Trading Estate Southgrove HS14 6PW	Invoice 2312844 Lift Easy Ltd Marchfields Park Laycaster LA14 7PL		Date: 01 April X6 VAT 020 5963 01 GB
			£
Fork lift truck	FL457	1	10,500.00
Attachment – tipping bin	1.2 cubic metre capacity	1	515.00
Warranty – 36 months		1	420.00
Net total			11,435.00
VAT @ 20%			2,237.00
Total			13,722.00

11435

AMBR took out a finance lease to cover this purchase.

The following information relates to the sale of an item of furniture no longer needed by the business:

Item ID	BSHLF14
Date of sale	30 September X6
Selling price excluding VAT	£300.00

AMBR Trading has a policy of capitalising expenditure over £500.

- Furniture and fittings are depreciated at 15% per year on a straight line basis.
- Machinery is depreciated at 25% per year on a diminishing balance basis.
- Depreciation is calculated on an annual basis and charged in equal instalments for each full month an asset is owned in the year

Complete the extract from the non-current assets register below for:

(a) Any acquisitions of non-current assets during the year ended 31 March 20X7
(b) Any disposals of non-current assets during the year ended 31 March 20X7
(c) Depreciation for the year ended 31 March 20X7.

Note: Not every cell will require an entry, and not all cells will accept entries. Show your answers to 2 decimal places.

Extract from non-current assets register

Description/ serial number	Acquisition date	Cost £	Depreciation charges £	Carrying amount £	Funding method	Disposal proceeds £	Disposal date
Furniture and fittings							
FICAB101	01/12/X5	690.00			Cash		
Year end 31/03/X6			34.50	655.50			
Year end 31/03/X7			103.50	552.00			
BSHLF14	01/10/X4	580.00			Cash		
Year end 31/03/X5			43.50	536.50			
Year end 31/03/X6			87.00	449.50			
Year end 31/03/X7			[A] 43.50 ▼	[B] 106 ▼		300.00 3 osep	
Machinery							
Jacking machine JMACH57	01/04/X4	8,080.00			Part-exchange		
Year end 31/03/X5			2,020.00	6,060.00			
Year end 31/03/X6			1,515.00	4,545.00			
Year end 31/03/X7			1136.25	3408.75			
[C] fork lift truck ▼	01/04/x6	11015	2753.75	8261.25	[D] Finance lease ▼		
Year end 31/03/X7							

Picklist:

[A]: 87.00, 67.43, 43.50, Nil.
[B]: 406.00, 382.07, 362.50, Nil
[C]: BSHLF14, FICAB101, Fork lift truck and tip bin FL457, Jacking machine JMACH57
[D]: Loan, Hire purchase, Finance lease

..

Task 1.2

This task is about recording non-current asset information in the general ledger, and other non-current asset matters.

- You are working on the accounts of a business that is registered for VAT.

- The financial year end is 31 March 20X7.

- A new vehicle has been acquired. VAT can be reclaimed on this vehicle.

- The cost excluding VAT was £15,300; this was paid from the bank.

- The residual value is expected to be £4,500 excluding VAT. It is estimated it will be used for three years.

- Vehicles are depreciated on a straight line basis. A full year's depreciation is applied in the year of acquisition.

- Depreciation has already been entered into the accounts for existing vehicles.

(a)   Calculate the depreciation charge for the year on the new vehicle.

£	3600

$$\frac{15,800 - 4,500}{3}$$

Make entries to account for:

(b)   The purchase of the new vehicle
(c)   The depreciation charge on the new vehicle

On each account, show clearly the balance carried down or transferred to the income statement account in the general ledger, as appropriate.

Vehicles at cost

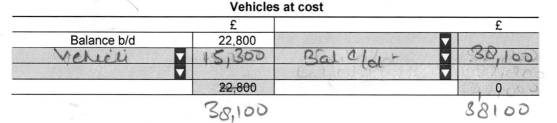

	£			£
Balance b/d	22,800		▼	
Vehicle ▼ ▼	15,300	Bal C/d ▼ ▼		38,100
	22,800			0

38,100   38100

Depreciation charges

	£		£
Balance b/d	6,400		
Acc·dep	3600	$P L	10,000
	6,400		0
	10,000		10,000

Vehicles accumulated depreciation

	£		£
		Balance b/d	12,800
Bal c/d - 16400		dep charge -	3600
	16400		12,800
			16400

Picklist:

Balance b/d
Balance c/d
Bank
Depreciation charges
Disposals
Income statement account
Purchases
Purchases ledger control
Sales
Sales ledger control
Vehicle running expenses
Vehicles accumulated depreciation
Vehicles at cost
<Empty>

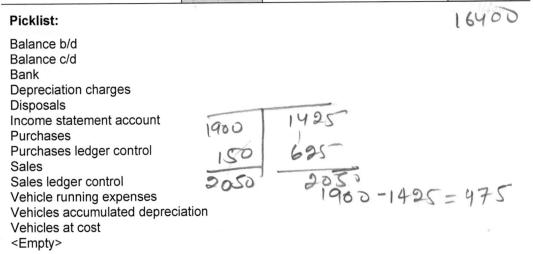

1900	1425
150	625
2050	2050

1900 - 1425 = 475

The business has sold a piece of machinery which had an original cost of £1,900. The accumulated depreciation on the machinery was £1,425 and a gain was made of £150 on its disposal.

(d) What were the sale proceeds of the machinery? Ignore VAT.

£ | 625

You are now working on the accounting records at a partnership business. This business needs to develop a policy for authorisation of new vehicle purchases.

(e) Which ONE of the following is the most suitable policy?

New vehicle purchases should be authorised by:

A partner of the business ☑

The driver of the vehicle ☐

An accounting technician ☐

Section 2

Task 2.1

This task is about accounting for accrued and prepaid income and expenses.

You are working on the accounts of a business for the year ended 31 March 20X7. In this task, you can ignore VAT.

You have the following information:

- The balance on the commission receivable account at the beginning of the financial year is £2,350.

- This is the commission receivable that was accrued at the end of the year on 31/03/X6.

- The bank summary for the year shows receipts for commission receivable of £28,900.

- The commission receivable account has been adjusted for commission of £1,900 relating to the month of March 20X7 but received after the year end.

- Double entry accounting is done in the general ledger.

(a) **Which of the following shows how the general ledger account for commission receivable looked at the beginning of the financial year? Tick the correct answer.**

Commission receivable

		£			£	
			01/04/X6	Accrued income	2,350	☐

Commission receivable

		£			£	
			01/04/X7	Accrued income	2,350	☐

Commission receivable

		£			£	
01/04/X6	Accrued income	2,350				☑

Commission receivable

		£			£	
01/04/X7	Accrued income	2,350				☐

131

(b) Complete the following statement:

On 31/03/X7, the commission receivable account shows an adjustment for

accrued income/pre-paid income of £ _1900_ credit/debit .

(c) Calculate the commission receivable for the year ended 31/03/X7.

£ _28,450_

The bank summary for the year shows payments for selling expenses of £12,800.

(d) Update the selling expenses account for this, showing clearly the balance to be carried down.

Selling expenses

	£		£
Bank –	12 800	Balance b/d	504
		SPL – 12296	12296
	0		504

_12,800_   _12,800_

Picklist:

Accrued expenses
Accrued income
Balance b/d
Balance c/d,
Bank,
Commission receivable
Income statement account
Prepaid expenses
Prepaid income
Purchases
Purchases ledger control account
Sales
Sales ledger control account
Selling expenses
<Empty>

Before transferring the balance on the selling expenses account to the income statement you find that the payments figure for selling expenses included £900 relating to the period 01/02/X7 to 31/07X7.

$$\frac{900}{6} = 150 \times 4 = 600$$

(e) Complete the following statement:

An adjustment of £ _600·00_ needs to be made, which will increase/decrease the selling expenses for the year ended 31/03/X7.

....

$$\frac{900}{7} = 128.6$$

BPP
LEARNING MEDIA

Task 2.2

This task is about preparing a trial balance.

You are working on the accounts of a business with a year end of 31 March. You have five extracts from the ledger accounts as at 31 March 20X7. You need to start preparing the trial balance as at 31 March 20X7.

Using all the information given below and the figures given in the table, enter amounts in the appropriate trial balance columns for the accounts shown.

Do NOT enter zeros in unused column cells.

Do NOT enter any figures as negatives.

Allowance for doubtful debts adjustment

		£			£
31/03/X7	Balance b/f	502			

Disposal of non-current asset

		£			£
			31/03/X7	Balance b/f	375

Office costs

		£			£
31/03/X7	Balance b/f	4,480			

Included in this balance is an amount for accrued expenses of £280 as at 31/03/X7.

Recycling rebates

		£			£
			31/03/X7	Balance b/f	7,360

Included in this balance is an amount for accrued income of £450 as at 31/03/X7.

VAT

		£			£
			31/03/X7	Balance b/f	1,845

Extract from the trial balance as at 31 March 20X7:

Account	Ledger balance £	Trial balance £ Dr	Trial balance £ Cr
Accrued expenses		200	
Accrued income			480
Advertising costs	2,900	2900	
Allowance for doubtful debts adjustment		502	
Depreciation charges	867	867	
Disposal of non-current asset			375
Fixtures and fittings at cost	6,800	6800	
Office costs		4480	
Recycling rebates			7360
VAT			1845

There were no accruals or prepayments of expenses and income other than those stated.

••

Task 2.3

This task is about recording adjustments in the extended trial balance and closing off accounts.

You are working on the accounts of a business with a year end of 31 March. A trial balance has been drawn up and a suspense account opened.

You now need to make some corrections and adjustments for the year ended 31 March 20X7. You may ignore VAT in this task.

(a) Record the adjustments needed in the extract from the extended trial balance to deal with the items below. You will not need to enter adjustments on every line. DO NOT enter zeros into unused cells.

(i) A bank payment of £860 made on 25 March 20X7 for vehicle insurance for the year ended 31 March 20X8 is included in the insurance expenses figure as at 31 March 20X7.

(ii) Travel expenses of £510 paid by business debit card have been correctly entered into the travel expenses account but no other entries were made.

(iii) The allowance for doubtful debts needs to be adjusted to 4% of the outstanding trade receivables.

(iv) On 21 March 20X7, a customer account was settled by prompt payment which meant that a discount was allowed.

Customer account balance	£1,000
Discount allowed	£15
Bank receipt	£985

When posting the figures, the entry for discounts was omitted. The other entries were made correctly.

Extract from extended trial balance

Ledger account	Ledger balances		Adjustments	
	Dr £	Cr £	Dr £	Cr £
Accrued expenses		860		
Administration expenses	12,790			
Allowance for doubtful debts		750	62	
Allowance for doubtful debts - adjustment				62
Bank		1,690		50
Discounts allowed	1,740		15	
Insurance expenses	1,080			860
Irrecoverable debts	260			
Prepaid expenses			860	
Purchases	94,600			
Purchases ledger control account		11,140		
Sales		159,000		
Sales ledger control account	17,200			
Suspense		495	860	15
Travel expenses	7,310			

$$17,200 \times \frac{4}{100} = 688$$

The ledgers are now ready to be closed off for the year ended 31 March 20X7.

(b) Show the correct journal entries to close off the administration expenses account and select an appropriate narrative.

Journal

	Dr £	Cr £
Administration Expenses ▼	✓	✓
SPL (12,790 ▼	✓	✓

Picklist:

Accrued expenses
Administration expenses
Allowance for doubtful debts
Allowance for doubtful debts – adjustment
Bank
Discounts allowed
Income statement account
Insurance expenses
Irrecoverable debts
Prepaid expenses
Purchases
Purchases ledger control account
Sales
Sales ledger control account
Statement of financial position
Suspense
Travel expenses
<Empty>

Narrative

▼

Picklist:

Transfer of administration expenses for year ended 31 March 20X7 to the statement of financial position

Transfer of administration expenses for the year ended 31 March 20X7 to the bank account

Transfer of administration expenses for the year ended 31 March 20X7 to the suspense account

Transfer of administration expenses for the year ended 31 March 20X7 to the income statement

Task 2.4

This task is about completing an extended trial balance.

You have the following extended trial balance. The adjustments have already been correctly entered.

Extend the figures into the income statement and statement of financial position columns. Do NOT enter zeros into unused column cells. Make the columns balance by entering figures and a label in the correct places.

Extended trial balance

Ledger account	Ledger balances		Adjustments		Income statement		Statement of financial position	
	Dr £	Cr £	Dr £	Cr £	Dr £	Cr £	Dr £	Cr £
Allowance for doubtful debts		1,300	300					*1000*
Allowance for doubtful debts adjustment				300	*300*			
Bank	28,380			500			*27,880*	
Capital		4,530						*4530*
Closing inventory			30,000	30,000		*30,000*	*30,000*	
Depreciation charges			15,500		*15,500*			
Office expenses	69,550			500	*69050*			
Opening inventory	26,000				*26,000*			
Payroll expenses	31,150			150	*31,000*			
Purchases	188,000		900		*188,900*			
Purchases ledger control account		29900						*29900*
Sales		436,000				*436,000*		
Sales ledger control account	36,000						*36,000*	
Selling expenses	67,000				*67,000*			
Suspense		250	1150	900				
VAT		9,800						*9,800*
Vehicles at cost	62,000						*62,000*	
Vehicles accumulated depreciation		26,300		15,500				*41800*
Bal c/d ▼						*60,050*		
	508,080	508,080	47,850	47,850	*397450* *350*	*461300*	*1155880* *155880*	*1155880*

Picklist:

Loss
Profit
<Empty>

87030

Task 2.5

This task is about preparing reconciliations.

The bank statement has been compared with the cash book and the following differences identified:

1   Bank interest paid of £62 was not entered into the cash book.

2   A cheque payment for £450 has been incorrectly entered in the cash book as £540.

3   Cheques totalling £2,980 paid into the bank at the end of the month are not showing on the bank statement.

4   A BACS receipt of £3,200 from a customer has not been entered in the cash book.

The balance showing on the bank statement is a credit of £4,628 and the balance in the cash book is a debit of £4,380.

Use the following table to show the THREE adjustments you need to make to the cash book.

Adjustment	Amount £	Debit	Credit
① Bank Interest ▼	62	62	62
② cheque Payment ▼	90	90	90
③ Bacs receipt ▼	3200	3,200	

Picklist:

Adjustment for (1)
Adjustment for (2)
Adjustment for (3)
Adjustment for (4)
<Empty>

[handwritten workings:] 4380 | 62 3900 | 90 Bac 7428

[handwritten workings:] 90 62 152

Task 2.6

The task is to test your knowledge.

(a)   Why do businesses keep a subsidiary purchases ledger? Choose the ONE m suitable reason:

To summarise the total purchases for the business.

To show how much suppliers are owed in total.

To show how much each individual supplier is owed.

To enable the production of individual customer statements.

You have been asked to reconcile the cash book to the bank statement.

(b)   What can this reconciliation show?

That a cheque receipt from a customer has been posted to the purchases ledger.

That a cheque sent to a supplier has not been banked.

That a BACS payment has been sent to the wrong supplier bank account.

That a direct debit payment taken by a supplier has been recorded in the wrong general ledger account.

BPP LEARNING MEDIA

AAT PRACTICE ASSESSMENT 1
ACCOUNTS PREPARATION I

ANSWERS

Section 1

Task 1.1

Extract from non-current assets register

Description/ serial sumber	Acquisition Date	Cost £	Depreciation charges £	Carrying amount £	Funding method	Disposal proceeds £	Disposal date
Furniture and fittings							
FICAB101	01/12/X5	690.00			Cash		
Year end 31/03/X6			34.50	655.50			
Year end 31/03/X7			103.50	552			
BSHLF14	01/10/X4	580.00			Cash		
Year end 31/03/X5			43.50	536.50			
Year end 31/03/X6			87.00	449.50			
Year end 31/03/X7			43.50	Nil		300	30/09/X6
Machinery							
Jacking machine JMACH57	01/04/X4	8,080.00			Part-exchange		
Year end 31/03/X5			2,020.00	6,060.00			
Year end 31/03/X6			1,515.00	4,545.00			
Year end 31/03/X7			1,136.25	3,408.75			
Fork lift truck and tip bin FL457	01/04/X6	11,015			Finance lease		
Year end 31/03/X7			2,753.75	8,261.25			

Task 1.2

(a) Calculate the depreciation charge for the year on the new vehicle.

£ | 3,600

(b) – (c)

Vehicles at cost

	£		£
Balance b/d	22,800	Balance c/d	38,100
Bank	15,300		
	38,100		38,100

Depreciation charge

	£		£
Balance b/d	6,400	Income statement account	10,000
Vehicles accumulated depreciation	3,600		
	10,000		10,000

Vehicles accumulated depreciation

	£		£
Balance c/d	16,400	Balance b/d	12,800
		Depreciation charges	3,600
	16,400		16,400

(d) What were the sale proceeds of the machinery? Ignore VAT.

£ | 625

(e) Which ONE of the following is the most suitable policy?

New vehicle purchases should be authorised by:

A partner of the business	✓
The driver of the vehicle	☐
An accounting technician	☐

Task 2.4

This task is about completing an extended trial balance.

You have the following extended trial balance. The adjustments have already been correctly entered.

Extend the figures into the income statement and statement of financial position columns. Do NOT enter zeros into unused column cells. Make the columns balance by entering figures and a label in the correct places.

Extended trial balance

Ledger account	Ledger balances		Adjustments		Income statement		Statement of financial position	
	Dr £	Cr £	Dr £	Cr £	Dr £	Cr £	Dr £	Cr £
Allowance for doubtful debts		1,300	300					1,000
Allowance for doubtful debts adjustment				300	300			
Bank	28,380			500			27,880	
Capital		4,530						4,530
Closing inventory			30,000	30,000		30,000	30,000	
Depreciation charges			15,500		15,500			
Office expenses	69,550			500	69,050			
Opening inventory	26,000				26,000			
Payroll expenses	31,150			150	31,000			
Purchases	188,000		900		188,900			
Purchases ledger control account		29900						29900
Sales		436,000				436,000		
Sales ledger control account	36,000						36,000	
Selling expenses	67,000				67,000			
Suspense		250	1150	900				
VAT		9,800						9,800
Vehicles at cost	62,000						62,000	
Vehicles accumulated depreciation		26,300		15,500				41,800
▼						bal c/a 60,850		
	508,080	508,080	47,850	47,850	397,450	461,300	155,880	155,880

Picklist:

Loss
Profit
<Empty>

87030

Task 2.5

This task is about preparing reconciliations.

The bank statement has been compared with the cash book and the following differences identified:

1   Bank interest paid of £62 was not entered into the cash book.

2   A cheque payment for £450 has been incorrectly entered in the cash book as £540.

3   Cheques totalling £2,980 paid into the bank at the end of the month are not showing on the bank statement.

4   A BACS receipt of £3,200 from a customer has not been entered in the cash book.

The balance showing on the bank statement is a credit of £4,628 and the balance in the cash book is a debit of £4,380.

Use the following table to show the THREE adjustments you need to make to the cash book.

Adjustment		Amount £	Debit	Credit
① Bank Interest ▼		62	62	62
② cheque Payment ▼		90	90	90
③ Bacs receipt ▼		3200	3,200	

Picklist:

Adjustment for (1)
Adjustment for (2)
Adjustment for (3)
Adjustment for (4)
<Empty>

handwritten notes: 4380 | 62 ; 3200 | 24 ; Bal c/o 7420 ; 90 / 62 / 152

Task 2.6

The task is to test your knowledge.

(a) Why do businesses keep a subsidiary purchases ledger? Choose the ONE most suitable reason:

To summarise the total purchases for the business. ☐

To show how much suppliers are owed in total. ☐

To show how much each individual supplier is owed. ☑

To enable the production of individual customer statements. ☐

You have been asked to reconcile the cash book to the bank statement.

(b) What can this reconciliation show?

That a cheque receipt from a customer has been posted to the purchases ledger. ☐

That a cheque sent to a supplier has not been banked. ☑

That a BACS payment has been sent to the wrong supplier bank account. ☒

That a direct debit payment taken by a supplier has been recorded in the wrong general ledger account. ☐

AAT PRACTICE ASSESSMENT 1
ACCOUNTS PREPARATION I

ANSWERS

Section 1

Task 1.1

Extract from non-current assets register

Description/ serial sumber	Acquisition Date	Cost £	Depreciation charges £	Carrying amount £	Funding method	Disposal proceeds £	Disposal date
Furniture and fittings							
FICAB101	01/12/X5	690.00			Cash		
Year end 31/03/X6			34.50	655.50			
Year end 31/03/X7			103.50	552			
BSHLF14	01/10/X4	580.00			Cash		
Year end 31/03/X5			43.50	536.50			
Year end 31/03/X6			87.00	449.50			
Year end 31/03/X7			43.50	Nil		300	30/09/X6
Machinery							
Jacking machine JMACH57	01/04/X4	8,080.00			Part-exchange		
Year end 31/03/X5			2,020.00	6,060.00			
Year end 31/03/X6			1,515.00	4,545.00			
Year end 31/03/X7			1,136.25	3,408.75			
Fork lift truck and tip bin FL457	01/04/X6	11,015			Finance lease		
Year end 31/03/X7			2,753.75	8,261.25			

Task 1.2

(a) Calculate the depreciation charge for the year on the new vehicle.

£ | 3,600

(b) – (c)

Vehicles at cost

	£		£
Balance b/d	22,800	Balance c/d	38,100
Bank	15,300		
	38,100		38,100

Depreciation charge

	£		£
Balance b/d	6,400	Income statement account	10,000
Vehicles accumulated depreciation	3,600		
	10,000		10,000

Vehicles accumulated depreciation

	£		£
Balance c/d	16,400	Balance b/d	12,800
		Depreciation charges	3,600
	16,400		16,400

(d) What were the sale proceeds of the machinery? Ignore VAT.

£ | 625

(e) Which ONE of the following is the most suitable policy?

New vehicle purchases should be authorised by:

A partner of the business	✓
The driver of the vehicle	
An accounting technician	

Section 2

Task 2.1

(a) Which of the following shows how the general ledger account for commission receivable looked at the beginning of the financial year? Tick the correct answer.

Commission receivable

		£			£	
			01/04/X6	Accrued income	2,350	☐

Commission receivable

		£			£	
			01/04/X7	Accrued income	2,350	☐

Commission receivable

		£			£	
01/04/X6	Accrued income	2,350				✓

Commission receivable

		£			£	
01/04/X7	Accrued income	2,350				☐

(b) Complete the following statement:

On 31/03/X7, the commission receivable account shows an adjustment for  accrued income of £ 1,900 credit .

(c) Calculate the commission receivable for the year ended 31/03/X7.

£	28,450

The bank summary for the year shows payments for selling expenses of £12,800.

(d) Update the selling expenses account for this, showing clearly the balance to be carried down.

Selling expenses

	£		£
Bank	12,800	Balance b/d	504
		Balance b/d	12,296
	12,800		12,800

Before transferring the balance on the selling expenses account to the income statement you find that the payments figure for selling expenses included £900 relating to the period 01/02/X7 to 31/07X7.

(e) Complete the following statement:

An adjustment of £ | 600 | needs to be made, which will | decrease | the selling expenses for the year ended 31/03/X7.

Task 2.2

Extract from the trial balance as at 31 March 20X7:

	Ledger balance	Trial balance	
Account	**£**	**£ Dr**	**£ Cr**
Accrued expenses			280
Accrued income		450	
Advertising costs	2,900	2,900	
Allowance for doubtful debts adjustment		502	
Depreciation charges	867	867	
Disposal of non-current asset			375
Fixtures and fittings at cost	6,800	6,800	
Office costs		4,480	
Recycling rebates			7,360
VAT			1,845

Task 2.3

Extract from extended trial balance

Ledger account	Ledger balances		Adjustments	
	Dr £	Cr £	Dr £	Cr £
Accrued expenses		860		
Administration expenses	12,790			
Allowance for doubtful debts		750	62	
Allowance for doubtful debts - adjustment				62
Bank		1,690		510
Discounts allowed	1,740		15	
Insurance expenses	1,080			860
Irrecoverable debts	260			
Prepaid expenses			860	
Purchases	94,600			
Purchases ledger control account		11,140		
Sales		159,000		
Sales ledger control account	17,200			
Suspense		495	510	15
Travel expenses	7,310			

(b) Show the correct journal entries to close off the administration expenses account and select an appropriate narrative.

Journal

	Dr £	Cr £
Administration expenses		12,790
Income statement account	12,790	

Narrative

Transfer of administration expenses for year ended 31 March 20X7 to the income statement	▼

Task 2.4

Extended trial balance

Ledger account	Ledger balances		Adjustments		Income statement		Statement of financial position	
	Dr £	Cr £	Dr £	Cr £	Dr £	Cr £	Dr £	Cr £
Allowance for doubtful debts		1,300	300					1,000
Allowance for doubtful debts adjustment				300		300		
Bank	28,380			500				
Capital		4,530						4,530
Closing inventory			30,000	30,000		30,000	30,000	
Depreciation charges			15,500		15,500			
Office expenses	69,550			500	69,050			
Opening inventory	26,000				26,000			
Payroll expenses	31,150			150	31,000			
Purchases	188,000			900	188,900			
Purchases ledger control account		29900						29,900
Sales		436,000				436,000		
Sales ledger control account	36,000						36,000	
Selling expenses	67,000				67,000			
Suspense		250	1150	900				
VAT		9,800						9,800
Vehicles at cost	62,000						62,000	
Vehicles accumulated depreciation		26,300		15,500				41,800
Profit ▼					68,850			68,850
	508,080	508,080	47,850	47,850	466,300	466,300	155,880	155,880

Task 2.5

Adjustment	Amount £	Debit	Credit
Adjustment for (1)	62		✓
Adjustment for (2)	90	✓	
Adjustment for (4)	3,200	✓	

Task 2.6

(a) Why do businesses keep a subsidiary purchases ledger? Choose the ONE most suitable reason:

To summarise the total purchases for the business. ☐

To show how much suppliers are owed in total. ☐

To show how much each individual supplier is owed. ☑

To enable the production of individual customer statements. ☐

You have been asked to reconcile the cash book to the bank statement.

(b) What can this reconciliation show?

That a cheque receipt from a customer has been posted to the purchases ledger. ☐

That a cheque sent to a supplier has not been banked. ☑

That a BACS payment has been sent to the wrong supplier bank account. ☐

That a direct debit payment taken by a supplier has been recorded in the wrong general ledger account. ☐

AAT PRACTICE ASSESSMENT 2
ACCOUNTS PREPARATION I

Time allowed: 2 hours

Section 1

Task 1.1

This task is about recording information for non-current assets for a business known as AMBR Trading. AMBR Trading is registered for VAT and has a financial year end of 31 March.

The following is a purchase invoice received by AMBR Trading relating to some items to be used in its office:

To: AMBR Trading Unit 6, East End Trading Estate, Southgrove HS14 6PW	Invoice CJL40698 Copyzee Sales Ltd 178 Judd Road Endsleigh EN62 8 SP	Quantity	Date: 29 December 20X6 Total
			£
Photocopier/Scanner – pre used item	Model COPTL56B	1	830.00
Ink and toner	CT56BBlack	2	80.00
Pre-delivery testing		1	60.00
First year general maintenance			75.00
Total			1,045.00
Delivery date: 29/12/X6			

900 (handwritten annotation)

AMBR paid £1,045.00 to Copyzee on 31 January 20X7 with £1,045.00 borrowed interest-free from a third party. This amount is to be repaid in full on 31 December 20X8.

The following information relates to the sale of a motor vehicle no longer required by the business:

Description	1.4 litre car. BL09 RST
Date of sale	23 February 20X7
Selling price	£1,700.00

- VAT can be ignored.
- AMBR Trading has a policy of capitalising expenditure over £400.
- Office equipment is depreciated at 20% per year on a straight line basis.
- Motor vehicles are depreciated at 25% per year on a diminishing balance basis.
- A full year's depreciation is applied in the year of acquisition and none in the year of disposal.

Record the following in the extract from the non-current assets register below:

(a) Any acquisitions of non-current assets during the year ended 31 March 20X7
(b) Any disposals of non-current assets during the year ended 31 March 20X7
(c) Depreciation for the year ended 31 March 20X7

Notes: Not every cell will require an entry, and not all cells will accept entries. Show your answers to 2 decimal places.

Extract from non-current assets register

Description/ serial number	Acquisition date	Cost £	Depreciation charges £	Carrying amount £	Funding method	Disposal proceeds £	Disposal date
Office equipment							
Laptop computer 0012	31/01/X6	740.00		-	Cash		
Year end 31I03/X6			148.00	592.00			
Year end 31/03/X7			148.00	444.00			
Photocopier James [A] ▼	29/12/X6	890.00	178.00	712.00	[B] ▼		
Year end 31/03/X7		89	178.00	712.00			
Motor Vehicles							
2.0 litre van AB08 CDR	01/03/X5	9,440.00			Part-exchange		
Year end 31/03/X5			2,360.00	7,080.00			
Year end 31/03/X6			1,770.00	5,310.00			
Year end 31/03/X7			1,327.50	3,982.50			
1.4 litre car BL09 RST	30/10/X4	4,400.00			Part-exchange		
Year end 31/03/X5			1,100.00	3,300.00			
Year end 31/03/X6			825.00	2,475.00			
Year end 31/03/X7			0.00 [C] ▼	0.00 [D] ▼		1700.00	03 Feb 20X7

BPP LEARNING MEDIA

Picklist:

[A]: Laptop computer 0012, Photocopier / Scanner, 2.0l van AB08 CDR,1.4l car BL09 RST
[B]: Cash, Loan, Hire purchase
[C]: 825.00, 618.75, 206.25, Nil
[D]: 1,650.00, 1856.25, 2,268.75, Nil

....

Task 1.2

This task is about recording non-current asset information in the general ledger, and other non-current asset matters.

You are working on the accounts of a business for the year ended 31 March 20X7.

- VAT can be ignored.
- A machine was part-exchanged on 1 August 20X6. ~~1 Aru 2022 - 31 Mr~~
- The original machine was bought for £8,600 on 14 October 20X2. ~~- 31 March 2003~~
  ~~1 Apr 08 — 31 March 2004~~
  ~~1 Apr 04 — 31 March 2005~~
- Depreciation is provided at 20% per year on a straight line basis.
- A full year's depreciation is applied in the year of acquisition and none in the year of disposal. ~~1 April 05 — 31 Nov 2006~~
  ~~1 Apr 2006 — 31 M 2007~~
- A part-exchange allowance of £1,450 was given.
- £9,080 was paid from the bank to complete the purchase of the new machine.

Make entries relating to the disposal: ~~41016~~

(a) **Complete the disposals account.**
(b) **Update the bank account.** ~~1526~~

On each account, show clearly the balance carried down or transferred to the income statement account in the general ledger, as appropriate.

Disposals

	£			£
~~Bal b/d~~	~~8600~~	~~Acc dep -~~		~~6880~~
		~~New asset~~		~~1,450~~
		~~SPL - Loss~~		~~350~~
	~~8600~~			~~8600~~

~~Machn~~
~~8,600~~

~~8600 x 20 = 1720 x~~
~~100~~
~~= 6880~~

~~New asset value 10,530~~

Bank

	£			£
Balance b/d	8,370	New asset ~~cost~~	▼	9080
Bal c/d -	▼ 710		▼	
	8,370		▼	0

(handwritten: 9810)

Picklist:

Balance b/d
Balance c/d,
Bank
Depreciation charges
Disposals
Income statement account
Machinery accumulated depreciation
Machinery at cost
Purchases
Purchases ledger control
Repairs and maintenance costs
Sales
Sales ledger control
<Empty>

(c) Calculate the total cost of the new machine

£ | 10,530

(d) What will be the carrying amount of the new machine as at 31 March 20X8?

£ | 6318

(handwritten working:)

$$10530 \times \frac{20}{100} = 2106 \times 2$$

42120

10530 - 4912

(handwritten working bottom left:)

Bal b/d 86
Plat 1450
Bank - 9080
19130

Disposal

4912

A c.

Section 2

Task 2.1

This task is about accounting for accrued and prepaid income and expenses.

You are working on the accounts of a business for the year ended 31 March 20X7.
In this task, you can ignore VAT.

You have the following information:

- The balance on the rent receivable account at the beginning of the financial year is £4,500. This represents a prepayment for rent receivable as at the end of the year on 31/03/X6.

- The bank summary for the year shows receipts for rent receivable of £18,900. 4800

- The rent receivable account has been correctly adjusted for £4,800 rent for the quarter ended 30 June 20X7 which was received into the bank on 21 March 20X7. 1600 ×
  3 -240

- Double entry accounting is done in the general ledger.

(a) **Complete the following statements:**

On 01/04/X6, the rent receivable account shows a [Credit ▼] balance of
£ [4500] :

Picklist:
Credit
Debit

On 31/03/X7, the rent receivable account shows an adjustment for
[Prepaid b) Closing bal c/a ▼] of £ [4800].

Picklist:
Accrued expenses
Accrued income
Prepaid expenses
Prepaid income

(b) **Calculate the rent receivable for the year ended 31/03/X7.**

£ [18600]

The bank summary for the year shows payments for selling expenses of £21,550.

(c) **Update the general expenses account for this, showing clearly the balance to be carried down.**

General expenses

	£		£
	21,550	Balance b/d	850
Bank ▼	21,550	Bal c/d - ▼	20,700
	0		850
	21,550		21,550

Picklist:

Accrued expenses
Accrued income
Balance b/d
Balance c/d
Bank
General expenses
Income statement account
Prepaid expenses
Prepaid income
Purchases
Purchases ledger control account
Rent receivable
Sales
Sales ledger control account
<Empty>

$$\frac{540}{3} = 180 \times 2 = 360$$

You now find out that there is an unpaid bill of £540 for power costs for the three months ended 31 May 20X7 that has not been included in the accounts. Power is classified under general expenses.

(d) Complete the following statements: *increase*

Adjusting for this will [increase ▼] the total general expense figure transferred to the income statement for the year.

The adjustment is £ [180] .

Picklist:

Decrease
Increase
Have no effect

General expenses will show as a [debit ▼] in the income statement account in the general ledger.

Picklist:

Debit
Credit

$$21550$$
$$Debit - 180$$
$$\overline{21730}$$

$$Bal\ b/d - 850$$
$$SPL - 20,880$$
$$\overline{21730}$$

Task 2.2

This task is about preparing a trial balance.

You are working on the accounts of a business with a year end of 31 March. You have five extracts from the ledger accounts as at 31 March 20X7. You need to start preparing the trial balance as at 31 March 20X7.

Using all the information given below and the figures given in the table, enter amounts in the appropriate trial balance columns for the accounts shown.

Do NOT enter zeros in unused column cells.

Do NOT enter any figures as negatives.

Bank

		£			£
			31/03/X7	Balance b/f	5,635

Disposal of non-current asset

		£			£
			31/03/X7	Balance b/f	325

Sundry income

		£			£
			31/03/X7	Balance b/f	2,485

This balance has been adjusted for prepaid income of £170 as at 31/03/X7.

Telecommunication costs

		£			£
31/03/X7	Balance b/f	1,960			

This balance has been adjusted for prepaid expenses of £238 as at 31/03/X7.

VAT

		£			£
			31/03/X7	Balance b/f	2,040

Extract from the trial balance as at 31 March 20X7:

Account	Ledger balance £	Trial balance £ Dr	Trial balance £ Cr
Bank			5635
Cleaning costs	840	840	
Discounts allowed	1,560	1560	
Disposal of non-current asset			325
Drawings	16,500	16,500	
Prepaid expenses			230
Prepaid income		170	
Sundry income		94	9485
Telecommunication costs		1960	
VAT			2040

(handwritten: 21030   10725)

There were no accruals or prepayments of expenses and income other than those stated.

....

Task 2.3

This task is about recording journal entries.

You are working on the accounts of a business with a year end of 31 March. A trial balance has been drawn up and a suspense account opened. You now need to make some corrections and adjustments for the year ended 31 March 20X7.

Record the journal entries in the general ledger to deal with the items below.

You should:

–   **remove any incorrect entries where appropriate**
–   **post the correct entries**

You do not need to give narratives.

Do NOT enter zeros into unused column cells.

(a)   **Selling expenses of £834 have been charged to the sales account in error. The other side of the entry was correct.**

Journal

		Dr £	Cr £
Sales account	▼	834	834
Selling expense	▼	834	

(b) Fuel costing £72 was purchased using a business debit card and correctly recorded in the travel expenses account. No other entry has been made. Ignore VAT.

Journal

		Dr £	Cr £
~~T~~ Suspense ▼		72	
~~Su~~ Bank ▼			72

(c) The allowance for doubtful debts needs to be adjusted to 5% of the outstanding trade receivables. The sales ledger control account has a balance of £16,900 at the year end. The balance on the allowance for doubtful debts account is £750.

Journal

		Dr £	Cr £
Allowance for dd Adjus ▼		95	
Allowan fur d.debts ▼			95

Picklist:

Accruals
Allowance for doubtful debts
Allowance for doubtful debts adjustment
Bank
General expenses
Prepayments
Purchases
Purchases ledger control account
Purchases returns
Sales
Sales ledger control account
Sales returns
Selling expenses
Suspense
Travel expenses
<Empty>

$$16,900 \times \frac{5}{100}$$
$$= 845 - 750$$
$$= 95$$

(d) The figures from the columns of the sales day book for 25 March 20X7 have been totalled correctly as follows:

Sales column	£1,700
Vat column	£340
Total column	£2,040

The amounts have been posted as follows:

Cr Sales	£1,700 *1632.*
Cr VAT	£340 *– 408*
Dr Sales ledger control account	£2,040

Journal

		Dr £	Cr £
VAT	▼	*340*	
Suspance	▼		*340*
VAT	▼		*340*
Suspence	▼	*340*	

Picklist:

Accruals
Allowance for doubtful debts
Allowance for doubtful debts adjustment
Bank
General expenses
Prepayments
Purchases
Purchases ledger control account
Purchases returns
Sales
Sales ledger control account
Sales returns
Selling expenses
Suspense
VAT
<Empty>

Task 2.4

You have the following extended trial balance. The adjustments have already been correctly entered.

Extend the figures into the income statement and statement of financial position columns. Do NOT enter zeros into unused column cells. Make the columns balance by entering figures and a label in the correct places.

Extended trial balance

Ledger account	Ledger balances Dr £	Ledger balances Cr £	Adjustments Dr £	Adjustments Cr £	Income statement Dr £	Income statement Cr £	Statement of financial position Dr £	Statement of financial position Cr £
Accruals								
Bank	7,129						7129	
Capital		16,000		6,000				22000
Cash	425			200			225	
Closing inventory			5,900	5,900		5,900	5900	
Depreciation charges	2,790				2790			
Drawings			6,000				6000	
Fixtures and fittings at cost	18,600						18,600	
Fixtures and fittings - accumulated depreciation		8,370						8370
General expenses	4,850		170		5020			
Interest received		146		36		182		
Opening inventory	5,180				5182			
Purchases	37,400		200		37,600			
Purchases ledger control account		4,867	145					4722
Rent	7,200				7200			
Sales		69,300				69,300		
Suspense	109		36	145				
Wages	15,000				15,000			
P/L Bal₆-2598					Bal₆-2598			
TOTAL	98,683	98,683	12,451	12,451	0 72,790	0 75382	0 37,954	0 35092

Picklist:

Profit
Loss
<Empty>

Task 2.5

SLCA = 14,950
SL = 12,394

This task is about preparing reconciliations.

The individual balances of the accounts in the sales ledger have been listed and totalled to £14,950. The total has been compared with the £12,394 balance on the sales ledger control account. After investigation the following errors were found:

1   A sales invoice of £540 has been posted to Customer A's account in the sales ledger, rather than Customer B.

2   Cheques of £3,056 received from customers have not been recorded in the individual accounts.

3   A customer account with a debit balance of £2,800 has been listed in the sales ledger as £2,080.

4   A credit note issued for £110 has been debited to a customer account.

Use the following table to show the THREE adjustments required to the listing of sales ledger balances.

Adjustment		Amount £	Add	Deduct
(1) Cheque	▼	3056		✓
(3) customer a/c	▼	720	720	
(2) Credit note -	▼	110		✓

Picklist:

Adjustment for (1)
Adjustment for (2)
Adjustment for (3)
Adjustment for (4)
<Empty>

2800 | 2080
720

12,394 | 540 | 650
720 | 110

1 3114

12,394 | 3056
720 | 110 | 3166
13114 | 3166

BPP
LEARNING MEDIA

Task 2.6

The task is to test your knowledge.

(a) Which of these statements is true? Choose ONE:

The weighted average cost method of inventory valuation is the only method acceptable under accounting standards. ☐

Marketing costs may be included in the cost of inventory. ☐

Inventories may include raw materials purchased for making into products for sale. ☑

Inventory is valued at the higher of cost and net realisable value. ☐

A business has a financial year end of 31 March. In September 20X6, it renews its insurance premiums for the twelve months ended 30 September 20X7 with a single payment from the bank account.

The accountant splits the amount equally between the financial years ended 31 March 20X7 and 20X8.

(b) Which ONE of the following accounting principles best explains why the accountant has done this?

31 March .

Accruals ☑

Consistency ☐

Going concern ☐

Prudence ☐

AAT PRACTICE ASSESSMENT 2
ACCOUNTS PREPARATION I

ANSWERS

Section 1

Task 1.1

Extract from non-current assets register

Description/ serial number	Acquisition date	Cost £	Depreciation charges £	Carrying amount £	Funding method	Disposal proceeds £	Disposal date
Office equipment							
Laptop computer 0012	31/01/X6	740.00			Cash		
Year end 31I03/X6			148.00	592.00			
Year end 31/03/X7			148	444			
Photocopier/Scanner	29/12/X6	890			Loan		
Year end 31/03/X7			178	712			
Motor Vehicles							
2.0 litre van AB08 CDR	01/03/X5	9,440.00			Part-exchange		
Year end 31/03/X5			2,360.00	7,080.00			
Year end 31/03/X6			1,770.00	5,310.00			
Year end 31/03/X7			1,327.50	3,982.50			
1.4 litre car BL09 RST	30/10/X4	4,400.00			Part-exchange		
Year end 31/03/X5			1,100.00	3,300.00			
Year end 31/03/X6			825.00	2,475.00			
Year end 31/03/X7			nil	nil		1,700	23/02/X7

Task 1.2

(a) – (b)

Disposals

	£		£
Machinery at cost	8,600	Machinery accumulated depreciation	6,800
▼		Machinery at cost ▼	1,450
▼		Income statement account ▼	270
▼		▼	
▼		▼	
	8,600		8,600

Bank

	£		£
Balance b/d	8,370	Machinery at cost	9,080
Balance b/d	710	▼	
▼		▼	
	9,080		9,080

(c) Calculate the total cost of the new machine

£ | 10,530

(d) What will be the carrying amount of the new machine as at 31 March 20X8?

£ | 6,318

Section 2

Task 2.1

(a) Complete the following statements:

On 01/04/X6, the rent receivable account shows a | credit | balance of £
 4,500 .

On 31/03/X7, the rent receivable account shows an adjustment for | prepaid income |
of £ | 4,800 | .

(b) Calculate the rent receivable for the year ended 31/03/X7.

£ | 18,600 |

The bank summary for the year shows payments for selling expenses of £21,550.

(c) **Update the general expenses account for this, showing clearly the balance to be carried down.**

General expenses

	£		£
Bank	21,550	Balance b/d	850
		Balance c/d	20,700
	21,550		21,550

You now find out that there is an unpaid bill of £540 for power costs for the three months ended 31 May 20X7 that has not been included in the accounts. Power is classified under general expenses.

(d) Complete the following statements:

Adjusting for this will | increase | the total general expense figure transferred to the income statement for the year.

The adjustment is £ | 180 | .

General expenses will show as a | debit | in the income statement account in the general ledger.

....

Task 2.2

Extract from the trial balance as at 31 March 20X7:

Account	Ledger balance £	Trial balance £ Dr	Trial balance £ Cr
Bank			5,635
Cleaning costs	840	840	
Discounts allowed	1,560	1,560	
Disposal of non-current asset			325
Drawings	16,500	16,500	
Prepaid expenses		238	
Prepaid income			170
Sundry income			2,485
Telecommunication costs		1,960	
VAT			2,040

Task 2.3

(a) **Selling expenses of £834 have been charged to the sales account in error. The other side of the entry was correct.**

Journal

	Dr £	Cr £
Selling expenses	834	
Sales		834

BPP LEARNING MEDIA

(b) Fuel costing £72 was purchased using a business debit card and correctly recorded in the travel expenses account. No other entry has been made. Ignore VAT.

Journal

	Dr £	Cr £
Suspense	72	
Bank		72

(c) The allowance for doubtful debts needs to be adjusted to 5% of the outstanding trade receivables. The sales ledger control account has a balance of £16,900 at the year end. The balance on the allowance for doubtful debts account is £750.

Journal

	Dr £	Cr £
Allowance for doubtful debts adjustment	95	
Allowance for doubtful debts		95

(d) The figures from the columns of the sales day book for 25 March 20X7 have been totalled correctly as follows:

Sales column	£1,700
Vat column	£340
Total column	£2,040

The amounts have been posted as follows:

Cr Sales	£1,700
Cr VAT	£340
Dr Sales ledger control account	£2,040

Journal

	Dr £	Cr £
VAT	304	
Suspense		304
VAT		340
Suspense	340	

Task 2.4

Ledger account	Ledger balances		Adjustments		Income statement		Statement of financial position	
	Dr £	Cr £	Dr £	Cr £	Dr £	Cr £	Dr £	Cr £
Accruals				170				170
Bank	7,129						7,129	
Capital		16,000		6,000				22,000
Cash	425			200			225	
Closing inventory			5,900	5,900		5,900	5,900	
Depreciation charges	2,790				2,790			
Drawings			6,000				6,000	
Fixtures and fittings at cost	18,600						18,600	
Fixtures and fittings - accumulated depreciation		8,370						8,370
General expenses	4,850		170		5,020			
Interest received		146		36		182		
Opening inventory	5,180				5,180			
Purchases	37,400			200	37,600			
Purchases ledger control account		4,867	145					4,722
Rent	7,200				7,200			
Sales		69,300				69,300		
Suspense	109		36	145				
Wages	15,000				15,000			
Profit					2,592			
TOTAL	98,683	98,683	12,451	12,451	72,382	75,382	37,854	37,854

72790

Task 2.5

Adjustment	Amount £	Add	Deduct
Adjustment for (2)	3,056		✓
Adjustment for (3)	720	✓	
Adjustment for (4)	220		✓

Task 2.6

The task is to test your knowledge.

(a) Which of these statements is true? Choose ONE:

The weighted average cost method of inventory valuation is the only method acceptable under accounting standards. ☐

Marketing costs may be included in the cost of inventory. ☐

Inventories may include raw materials purchased for making into products for sale. ☑

Inventory is valued at the higher of cost and net realisable value. ☐

A business has a financial year end of 31 March. In September 20X6, it renews its insurance premiums for the twelve months ended 30 September 20X7 with a single payment from the bank account.

The accountant splits the amount equally between the financial years ended 31 March 20X7 and 20X8.

(b) Which ONE of the following accounting principles best explains why the accountant has done this?

Accruals ☑

Consistency ☐

Going concern ☐

Prudence ☐

BPP PRACTICE ASSESSMENT 1
ACCOUNTS PREPARATION I

Time allowed: 2 hours

Section 1

Task 1.1

This task is about recording information for non-current assets for a business known as Rootle Ltd. Rootle Ltd is registered for VAT and its year-end is 30 September.

The following is a purchase invoice received by Rootle Ltd:

Fittings Supplies plc Unit 76 East Trading Estate Mendlesham ME2 9FG	Invoice 9032	Date:	20 June X5
To:	Rootle Ltd 14 Larkmead Road Mendlesham ME6 2PO		
Description	Item number	Quantity	£
Warehouse racking system	WR617	1	2000.00
Delivery and set-up charges		1	200.00
Specialist oil for racking @ £15.00 per litre		3 litres	45.00
Net			2245.00
VAT @ 20%			449.00
Total			2694.00
Settlement terms: strictly 30 days net.			

> 2200

The following information relates to the sale of an item of machinery:

Identification number	MC5267
Date of sale	22 June X5
Selling price excluding VAT	£3250.00

- Rootle Ltd's policy is to recognise items of capital expenditure over £200 as non-current assets.
- Furniture and fittings are depreciated at 25% using the straight line method. There are no residual values.
- Machinery is depreciated at 40% using the reducing balance method.
- A full year's depreciation is charged in the year of acquisition and none in the year of sale.

Record the following information in the non-current assets register below:

(a) **Any acquisitions of non-current assets during the year ended 30 September X5**
(b) **Any disposals of non-current assets during the year ended 30 September X5**
(c) **Depreciation for the year ended 30 September X5**

Non-current assets register

Description	Acquisition date	Cost £	Depreciation £	Carrying amount £	Funding method	Disposal proceeds £	Disposal date
Furniture and fittings							
Warehouse racking systems							
WR290							
Year end 30/09/X3	1/12/X2	6,000.00	1,500.00	4,500.00	Credit		
Year end 30/09/X4			1,500.00	3,000.00			
Year end 30/09/X5			1500.	1500			
Cogine house Racking CORGTI	20/06/2x5 2900·00		5				
Year end 30/09/X5	20/06/2x5	9200·0					
			550·0	1650·0	Credit		
Machinery							
MC5267					Cash		
Year end 30/09/X3	1/10/X2	7,500.00	3,000.00	4,500.00			
Year end 30/09/X4			1,800.00	2,700.00		3250·00	22 June 20x5
Year end 30/09/X5			0·00	0·00			
MC5298					Credit		
Year end 30/09/X4	31/01/X4	8,800.00	3,520.00	5,280.00			
Year end 30/09/X5			2112·00	3168·0			

Task 1.2

This task is about recording non-current asset information in the general ledger and other non-current asset matters.

- You are working on the accounts of a sole trader who is registered for VAT. The business's year end is 31 December 20XX.

- On 1 September 20XX the business bought a new machine for the business on which VAT can be reclaimed.

- The machine cost £12,200 excluding VAT. An invoice has been received from the seller which has been recorded in the purchases day book.

- The machine's residual value is expected to be £2,300 excluding VAT.

- The business's depreciation policy for machines is 10% per annum on a straight line basis.

- Depreciation has already been entered into the accounts for the business's existing machines.

Make entries to account for:

(a) **The purchase of the new machine**
(b) **The depreciation on the new machine**

On each account, show clearly the balance carried down or transferred to the income statement.

Machines at cost

	£		£
Balance b/d	20,000		
Cost at the asset			

Machines accumulated depreciation

	£		£
		Balance b/d	8,600

Depreciation charge

	£		£
Balance b/d	5,700		

(c) When non-current assets are depreciated using the reducing balance method, an equal amount is charged for each year of the asset's life.

✓	
	True
✓	False

Section 2

Task 2.1

This task is about accounting for accruals and prepayments and preparing a trial balance.

You are working on the final accounts of a business for the year ended 30 June 20X4. In this task, you can ignore VAT.

You have the following information:

Balances as at:	1 July 20X3
	£
Accrual of rental income	250
Prepayment of selling expenses	87

$$\frac{270 \quad 90}{3}$$

The bank summary for the year shows receipts of rental income of £5,000. Included in this figure is £270 for the quarter ended 31 July 20X4.

(a) **Prepare the rental income account for the year ended 30 June 20X4 and close it off by showing the transfer to the income statement (profit and loss account).**

Rental income

Details	£	Details	£
Accrual Bal b/q.	250	Bank -	5000
Prepaid	90		
sp incone	4,660		
	5,000		5000

The bank summary for the year shows payments for selling expenses of £2,850. In June 20X4, £63 was paid for items delivered and used in July 20X4.

340

(b) **Prepare the selling expenses account for the year ended 30 June 20X4 and close it off by showing the transfer to the income statement. Include dates.**

Selling expenses

Date	Details	£	Date	Details	£
1/9	Bal b/d –	87		Prepayment	63
31	Bank –	2850		Prepaid	63
	Accrued –	62		SPL –	2874
		2937			2937

....

Task 2.2

This task is about preparing a trial balance.

You are working on the accounts of a business with a year end of 30 June. You have five extracts from the ledger accounts as at 30 June 20X4. You need to start preparing the trial balance as at 30 June 20X4.

Using all the information given below and the figures given in the table, enter amounts in the appropriate trial balance columns for the accounts shown.

Do NOT enter zeros in unused column cells.

Do NOT enter any figures as negatives.

Bank

		£			£
			30/06/X4	Balance b/f	10,460

Disposal of non-current asset

		£			£
			30/06/X4	Balance b/f	700

Interest received

		£			£
			30/06/X4	Balance b/f	3,250

This balance has been adjusted for interest received in advance of £240 as at 30/06/X4.

Telecommunication costs

		£			£
30/06/X4	Balance b/f	5,960			

This balance has been adjusted for prepaid expenses of £329 as at 30/06/X4.

VAT

		£			£
			30/06/X4	Balance b/f	7,230

Extract from trial balance as at 30 June 20X4

Account	£	Debit £	Credit £
Accrued expenses			
Accrued income			
Capital	10,000		10,000
Irrecoverable debts expense	780	780	
Discounts received	1,209		1,209
Interest expense	201	201	
Disposal of non-current asset			700
Bank			10460
Interest received			3250
Telecommunications costs		5960	
VAT			7930
Prepaid expenses		329	
Prepaid income			240

....

Task 2.3

This task is about recording journal entries.

You are working on the final accounts of a business with a year end of 31 December. A trial balance has been drawn up and a suspense account opened with a credit balance of £2,243. You now need to make some corrections and adjustments for the year ended 31 December 20X4.

Record the journal entries needed in the general ledger to deal with the items below.

You should:

−   **remove any incorrect entries, where appropriate**
−   **post the correct entries**

You do not need to give narratives.

Do NOT enter zeros into unused column cells.

Ignore VAT.

(a) Entries needed to increase the allowance for receivables from £1,524 to £2,887.

Journal

Account name	Debit £	Credit £
Allowance for dd debts		1363
Allowance for del adjust	1363	

(b) A fully depreciated vehicle has been sold for £1,986. Only the cash book has been updated for this transaction.

Journal

Account name	Debit £	Credit £
disposal		1986
Suspence	1986	

(c) Discounts received of £257 have only been entered into the purchases ledger control account from the cash payments book. |PLCA

Journal

Account name	Debit £	Credit £
Discount received		257
Suspance	257	257

(d) When posting from the purchases returns day book, the entries for credit notes totalling £459 have been made to the wrong sides of both the relevant accounts.

Journal

Account name	Debit £	Credit £
Purchase returns	459	459
PLCA	459	459
Purchase returns		459
PLCA	459	459

double the amount

Task 2.4

This task is about completing an extended trial balance.

You have the following extended trial balance. The adjustments have already been correctly entered.

Extend the figures into the income statement and statement of financial position columns.

Do NOT enter zeros into unused column cells.

Make the columns balance by entering figures and a label in the correct places.

Extended trial balance

Ledger account	Ledger balances		Adjustments		Income statement		Statement of financial position	
	£	£	£	£	£	£	£	£
Allowance for doubtful debts		1,347		203				1550
Allowance for doubtful debts adjustment			203		203	203		
Bank		5,290						5290
Capital		9,460						9460
Closing inventory			7,234	7,234		7234	7234	
Depreciation charge			7,800		7800			
Administration expenses	6,739			569	6170			
Opening inventory	9,933				9933			
Wages and salaries	29,378			6,000	23,378			
Purchases	34,289				34,289			
Purchases ledger control account		5,096						5096
Sales		112,015		3,000		115015		
Sales ledger control account	8,023						8023	
Marketing	7,365				7365			
Suspense		8,819	9,569	750				
VAT		6,300						6300
Machinery at cost	115,000		750		115750		115750	
Machinery accumulated depreciation		62,400		7,800				70200
					33111	9223 5257	5257	
	210,727	210,727	25,556	25,556	89138	122249	131067	97093

Task 2.5

This task is about preparing reconciliations.

The balance on the sales ledger control account has been compared with the total of the list of sales ledger accounts and the following differences have been identified:

1 The sales ledger column in the cash receipts book was undercast by £100 *reducing the balance.*

2 A contra for £76 was only recorded in the sales ledger

3 An invoice for £563 in the sales day book was not posted to the sales ledger

4 A total in the sales returns day book of £489 was recorded in the general ledger as £498 *-9. | 498*

The balance showing on the sales ledger control account is £5,097 and the total of the list of sales ledger balances is £4,367.

Use the following table to show the THREE adjustments you need to make to the sales ledger control account.

Adjustment	Amount £	Debit ✓	Credit ✓
1	100		✓
2	76	✓	✓
4	9	✓	✓

....

Task 2.6

This task is to test your knowledge. Choose ONE answer.

The rule for valuing inventory is to use

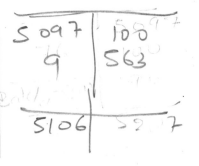

✓	
	The lower of FIFO and LIFO
✓	The lower of cost and net realisable value
	The lower of FIFO and net realisable value
	The lower of cost and LIFO

....

BPP PRACTICE ASSESSMENT 1
ACCOUNTS PREPARATION I

ANSWERS

Section 1

Task 1.1

(a) – (c)

Non-current assets register

Description	Acquisition date	Cost £	Depreciation £	Carrying amount £	Funding method	Disposal proceeds £	Disposal date
Furniture and fittings							
Warehouse racking systems							
WR290							
Year end 30/09/X3	1/12/X2	6,000.00	1,500.00	4,500.00	Credit		
Year end 30/09/X4			1,500.00	3,000.00			
Year end 30/09/X5			**1,500.00**	**1,500.00**			
	20/06/X5	**2,200.00**					
Year end 30/09/X5			**550.00**	**1,650.00**	**Credit**		
Machinery							
MC5267					Cash		
Year end 30/09/X3	1/10/X2	7,500.00	3,000.00	4,500.00			
Year end 30/09/X4			1,800.00	2,700.00			
Year end 30/09/X5						3,250.00	22/06/X5
MC5298					Credit		
Year end 30/09/X4	31/01/X4	8,800.00	3,520.00	5,280.00			
Year end 30/09/X5			**2,112.00**	**3,168.00**			

Task 1.2

(a) and (b)

Machines at cost

	£		£
Balance b/d	20,000	Balance c/d	32,200
Purchases ledger control	12,200		
	32,200		32,200

Machines accumulated depreciation

	£		£
Balance c/d	9,590	Balance b/d	8,600
		Depreciation charge	990
	9,590		9,590

Depreciation charge

	£		£
Balance b/d	5,700	Income statement	6,690
Machines accumulated depreciation	990		
	6,690		6,690

(c)

✓	
	True
✓	False

Section 2

Task 2.1

(a)

Rental income

Details	£	Details	£
Balance b/d	250	Bank	5,000
Balance c/d	90		
Income statement	4,660		
	5,000		5,000

(b)

Selling expenses

Date	Details	£	Date	Details	£
1/7	Balance b/d	87	30/6	Balance c/d	63
30/6	Bank	2,850	30/6	Income statement	2,874
		2,937			2,937

Task 2.2

Extract from trial balance as at 30 June 20X4

Account	£	Debit £	Credit £
Accrued expenses			
Accrued income			
Capital	10,000		10,000
Irrecoverable debts expense	780	780	
Discounts received	1,209		
Interest expense	201	201	
Disposal of non-current asset			700
Bank			10,460
Interest received			3,250
Telecommunications costs		5,960	
VAT			7,230
Prepaid expenses		329	
Prepaid income			240

Task 2.3

(a)

Journal

Account name	Debit £	Credit £
Allowance for doubtful debts adjustment	1,363	
Allowance for doubtful debts		1,363

(b)

Journal

Account name	Debit £	Credit £
Suspense account	1,986	
Disposals		1,986

(c)

Journal

Account name	Debit £	Credit £
Suspense account	257	
Discounts received		257

(d)

Journal

Account name	Debit £	Credit £
Purchases ledger control	459	
Purchases returns		459
Purchases ledger control	459	
Purchases returns		459

Task 2.4

Extended trial balance

Ledger account	Ledger balances		Adjustments		Income statement		Statement of financial position	
	£	£	£	£	£	£	£	£
Allowance for doubtful debts		1,347		203				1,550
Allowance for doubtful debts adjustment			203		203			
Bank		5,290						5,290
Capital		9,460						9,460
Closing inventory			7,234	7,234		7,234	7,234	
Depreciation charge			7,800		7,800			
Administration expenses	6,739			569	6,170			
Opening inventory	9,933				9,933			
Wages and salaries	29,378			6,000	23,378			
Purchases	34,289				34,289			
Purchases ledger control account		5,096						5,096
Sales		112,015		3,000		115,015		
Sales ledger control account	8,023						8,023	
Marketing	7,365				7,365			
Suspense		8,819	9,569	750				
VAT		6,300						6,300
Machinery at cost	115,000		750				115,750	
Machinery accumulated depreciation		62,400		7,800				70,200
Profit for the year					33,111			33,111
	210,727	210,727	25,556	25,556	**122,249**	**122,249**	**131,007**	**131,007**

Task 2.5

Adjustment	Amount £	Debit ✓	Credit ✓
Adjustment for 1	100		✓
Adjustment for 2	76		✓
Adjustment for 4	9	✓	

Task 2.6

✓	
	The lower of FIFO and LIFO
✓	The lower of cost and net realisable value
	The lower of FIFO and net realisable value
	The lower of cost and LIFO

BPP PRACTICE ASSESSMENT 2
ACCOUNTS PREPARATION I

Time allowed: 2 hours

Section 1

Task 1.1

This task is about recording information for non-current assets for a business known as Hagbourne & Co. The business is registered for VAT and its year end is 31 March.

The following is a purchase invoice received by Hagbourne & Co:

Office Supplies Ltd 28 High Street Cridley CR4 6AS	Invoice 198233	Date:	1 December 20X5
To:	Hagbourne & Co 67 Foggarty Street Cridley CR9 0TT		
Description	Item number	Quantity	£
Modular office workstation system	OFF783	1	3,500.00
Delivery and assembly charges		1	100.00
Printer paper		75 reams	200.00
Net			3,800.00
VAT @ 20%			760.00
Total			4,560.00
Settlement terms: strictly 30 days net.			

3,600

The following information relates to the sale of a motor vehicle:

Identification number	CR05 KJH
Date of sale	1 April 20X5
Selling price excluding VAT	£7,400.00

- Hagbourne & Co's policy is to recognise items of capital expenditure over £100 as non-current assets.

- Office equipment is depreciated at 20% per annum using the straight line method. A residual value of 25% of cost is assumed.

- Motor vehicles are depreciated at 40% per annum using the reducing balance method.

- A full year's depreciation is charged in the year of acquisition, none in the year of disposal.

Record the following information in the non-current assets register below:

(a) **Any acquisitions of non-current assets during the year ended 31 March 20X6**
(b) **Any disposals of non-current assets during the year ended 31 March 20X6**
(c) **Depreciation for the year ended 31 March 20X6**

Non-current assets register

Description	Acquisition date	Cost £	Depreciation £	Carrying amount £	Funding method	Disposal proceeds £	Disposal date
Motor vehicles							
CR04 YTR							
Year end 31/3/X4	1/4/X3	18,000.00	7,200.00	10,800.00	Credit		
Year end 31/3/X5			4,320.00	6,480.00			
Year end 31/3/X6			2592	3888			
CR05 KJH					Credit		
Year end 31/3/X5	1/4/X4	10,540.00	4,216.00	6,324.00			
Year end 31/3/X6			0.00	0.00		7,400.00	1 Apr/
Office equipment							
OFF253							
Year end 31/3/X4	1/1/X4	10,000.00	1,500.00	8,500.00	Cash		
Year end 31/3/X5			1,500.00	7,000.00			
Year end 31/3/X6			1500.0	5500			
OFF783	1/12/X5	3,600.0					
Year end 31/3/X6			540.0	3060.0			

(handwritten in left margin:) 10000 −2500 −7500

(handwritten at bottom:)

$$3600 - 900 = 2700 \times \frac{20}{100} = 540$$

BPP LEARNING MEDIA

Task 1.2

This task is about recording non-current asset information in the general ledger and other non-current asset matters.

- You are working on the accounts of a business which is not registered for VAT. The business's year end is 31 December 20X6.

- On 1 January 20X6 the business sold some machinery for £750. This amount has already been entered in the cash book.

- The machinery cost £2,000 on 1 January 20X3.

- The business's depreciation policy for machinery is 20% using the reducing balance method.

(a) Make entries to account for the disposal of the machine.

On each account, show clearly the balance carried down or transferred to the income statement.

Machines at cost

Balance b/d	15,000	disposal.	2000
Cost at cost	2000	Bal c/d	13,000
	15000		15000

Machines at cost

disposal acc	976	Balance b/d	9,200
Bal c/d -	8224		
	9200		9200

Disposal account

Cost at asset	2000	Acc dep -	976
		Bank -	750
		SPL - Loss	274
	2000		2000

1726

(b) **A non-current asset is disposed of and a part exchange allowance is given in respect of a new non-current asset. The amount of the allowance is:**

✓	
✓	Debited to the disposal account and credited to the non-current asset cost account
	Debited to the non-current asset cost account and credited to the disposal account

Section 2

Task 2.1

This task is about accounting for accruals and prepayments and preparing a trial balance.

You are working on the final accounts of a business for the year ended 30 September 20X6. In this task, you can ignore VAT.

You have the following information:

Balances as at:	1 October 20X5
	£
Prepayment of commission income	175
Accrual of stationery	134

The bank summary for the year shows receipts of commission income of £496. Commission of £63 is still due for September 20X6 at the year end.

(a) **Prepare the commission income account for the year ended 30 September 20X6 and close it off by showing the transfer to the income statement.**

Commission income

Details	£	Details	£
		Prepay Bal b/d -	175
SPL -	734	Bank -	496
		Accured incom	63

734 / 734

The bank summary for the year shows payments for stationery of £798. In September 20X6, £48 was paid for items delivered and used in October 20X6.

(b) **Prepare the stationery account for the year ended 30 September 20X6 and close it off by showing the transfer to the income statement. Include dates.**

Stationery

Date	Details	£	Date	Details	£
			1 Oct 20X5	Bal b/d -	134.
	Bank	798		Prepaid -	48
				SPL -	616
		798			798

182

Task 2.2

This task is about preparing a trial balance.

You are working on the accounts of a business with a year end of 30 September. You have five extracts from the ledger accounts as at 30 September 20X6. You need to start preparing the trial balance as at 30 September 20X6.

Using all the information given below and the figures given in the table, enter amounts in the appropriate trial balance columns for the accounts shown.

Do NOT enter zeros in unused column cells.

Do NOT enter any figures as negatives.

Allowance for doubtful debts adjustment

		£			£
30/09/X6	Balance b/f	230			

Disposal of non-current asset

		£			£
			30/09/X6	Balance b/f	500

Office costs

		£			£
30/09/X6	Balance b/f	3,660			

Included in this balance is an amount for accrued expenses of £420 as at 30I09/X6.

Recycling rebates

Recycling rebates

		£			£
			30/09/X6	Balance b/f	4,927

Included in this balance is an amount for accrued income of £750 as at 30I09/X6.

VAT

VAT

		£			£
			30/09/X6	Balance b/f	2,993

Extract from trial balance as at 30 September 20X6

Account	£	Debit £	Credit £
Accrued expenses		*420*	420
Accrued income		750	*750*
Drawings	2,500	2500	
Purchases returns	1,982		1982
Allowance for doubtful debts adjustment		230	
Disposal of non-current asset			500
Office costs		3660	
Recycling rebates			4997
VAT			9993
Prepaid expenses			
Prepaid income			

Task 2.3

This task is about recording adjustments in the extended trial balance and closing off accounts.

You are working on the final accounts of a business with a year end of 31 December 20X6. A trial balance has been drawn up and a suspense account opened with a debit balance of £3,526. You now need to make some corrections and adjustments for the year ended 31 December 20X6.

(a) **Record the adjustments needed on the extract from the extended trial balance to deal with the items below.**

You will not need to enter adjustments on every line. Do NOT enter zeros into unused cells.

(i) Entries need to be made for an irrecoverable debt of £672.

(ii) Drawings of £850 have been made. The correct entry was made in the cash book but no other entries were made.

(iii) Closing inventory for the year end 31 December 20X6 has not yet been recorded. Its value at cost is £9,350. Included in this figure are some items costing £345 that will be sold for £200.

(iv) Credit notes of £1,338 have been posted to the correct side of the sales ledger control account, but have been made to the same side of the sales returns account.

Sales return — 1338

207

Extract from extended trial balance

	Ledger balances		Adjustments	
	Debit £	Credit £	Debit £	Credit £
Allowance for doubtful debts adjustment		134		
Bank	7,826			
Closing inventory – SFP				
Closing inventory – income statement			9905	9205
Drawings			850	
Irrecoverable debts			672	
Plant and machinery – accumulated depreciation		19,800		
Purchases returns		2,781		
Purchases ledger control account		92,831		
Sales		169,200		
Sales returns	5,421		2671	
Sales ledger control account	12,569			
Suspense	3,526		2676	3526

(b) **The ledgers are ready to be closed off for the year ended 31 December 20X6. Show the correct entries to close off the allowance for doubtful debts adjustment account and insert an appropriate narrative.**

Account	Debit ✓	Credit ✓
Allowance for ddt adj	134	
SPL –		134

35 26 T

Task 2.4

This task is about completing an extended trial balance.

You have the following extended trial balance. The adjustments have already been correctly entered.

Extend the figures into the income statement and statement of financial position columns.

Do NOT enter zeros into unused column cells.

Make the columns balance by entering figures and a label in the correct places.

Extended trial balance

Ledger account	Ledger balances		Adjustments		Income statement		Statement of financial position	
	£	£	£	£	£	£	£	£
Bank	5,246						5246	
Capital		19,600						19,600
Closing inventory			6,712	6,712		6712	6712	
Depreciation charge	4,298		4,000		8298			
Discounts received		2,291		1,325		3616		
Drawings	11,712		9,826				21538	
Irrecoverable debts	627				627			
Motor expenses	2,065				2065			
Motor vehicles accumulated depreciation		12,500		4,000				16500
Motor vehicles at cost	20,000						20,000	
Office expenses	7,219				7,219			
Opening inventory	4,820				4,800			
Purchases	91,289				91,289			
Purchases ledger control account		7,109	786					6323
Salaries	32,781		3,484		36,265			
Sales		156,782				156,782		
Sales ledger control account	11,092						11,092	
Suspense	12,771		1,325	14,096				
VAT		5,638						5638
					16,527			16,597
	203,920	203,920	26,133	26,133	150583	167110	64508	64588

Task 2.5

This task is about preparing reconciliations.

The balance on the purchases ledger control account has been compared with the total of the list of purchases ledger accounts and the following differences have been identified:

1 Total discounts received of £1,489 were only recorded in the discounts received account   *PLCA =*

2 A purchases ledger column of £1,267 in the cash payments book was not posted to the purchases ledger control account

3 A contra for £123 was only recorded in the purchases ledger control account

4 The total column in the purchases returns day book was overcast by £180

The balance showing on the purchases ledger control account is £7,092 and the total of the list of purchases ledger balances is £4,639.

Use the following table to show the THREE adjustments you need to make to the purchases ledger control account.

Adjustment	Amount £	Debit ✓	Credit ✓
1	1489	1489	
2	1267	1267	
4	180		✓

Task 2.6

This task is to test your knowledge. Choose ONE answer.

To reduce the allowance for doubtful debts we must

✓	
	Credit the allowance for doubtful debts account
	Debit the irrecoverable debts account
✓	Credit the allowance for doubtful debts adjustment account
	Credit the sales ledger control account
	None of the above

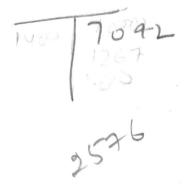

7092
1267
180

2576

BPP PRACTICE ASSESSMENT 2
ACCOUNTS PREPARATION I

ANSWERS

Section 1

Task 1.1

(a)-(b)

Non-current assets register

Description	Acquisition date	Cost £	Depreciation £	Carrying amount £	Funding method	Disposal proceeds £	Disposal date
Motor vehicles							
CR04 YTR							
Year end 31/3/X4	1/4/X3	18,000.00	7,200.00	10,800.00	Credit		
Year end 31/3/X5			4,320.00	6,480.00			
Year end 31/3/X6			2,592.00	3,888.00			
CR05 KJH					Credit		
Year end 31/3/X5	1/4/X4	10,540.00	4,216.00	6,324.00			
Year end 31/3/X6						7,400.00	1/4/X5
Office equipment							
OFF253							
Year end 31/3/X4	1/1/X4	10,000.00	1,500.00	8,500.00	Cash		
Year end 31/3/X5			1,500.00	7,000.00			
Year end 31/3/X6			1,500.00	5,500.00			
OFF783	1/12/X5	3,600.00					
Year end 31/3/X6			540.00	3,060.00			

Task 1.2

(a)

Machines at cost

Balance b/d	15,000	Disposal account	2,000
		Balance c/d	13,000
	15,000		15,000

Machines at cost

Disposal account	976	Balance b/d	9,200
Balance c/d	8,224		
	9,200		9,200

Disposal account

Machines at cost	2,000	Machines accumulated depreciation	976
		Bank	750
		Income statement	274
	2,000		2,000

(b)

✓	
	Debited to the disposal account and credited to the non-current asset cost account
✓	Debited to the non-current asset cost account and credited to the disposal account

Section 2

Task 2.1

(a)

Commission income

Details	£	Details	£
Income statement	734	Balance b/d	175
		Bank	496
	—	Balance c/d	63
	734		734

(b)

Stationery

Date	Details	£	Date	Details	£
30/9	Bank	798	1/10	Balance b/d	134
			30/9	Balance c/d	48
		—	30/9	Income statement	616
		798			798

Task 2.2

Extract from trial balance as at 30 September 20X6

Account	£	Debit £	Credit £
Accrued expenses			420
Accrued income		750	
Drawings	2,500	2,500	
Purchases returns	1,982		1,982
Allowance for doubtful debts adjustment		230	
Disposal of non-current asset			500
Office costs		3,660	
Recycling rebates			4,927
VAT			2,993
Prepaid expenses			
Prepaid income			

Task 2.3

(a)

Extract from extended trial balance

	Ledger balances		Adjustments	
	Debit £	Credit £	Debit £	Credit £
Allowance for doubtful debts adjustment		134		
Bank	7,826			
Closing inventory – SFP			9,205	
Closing inventory – income statement				9,205
Drawings			850	
Irrecoverable debts			672	
Plant and machinery – accumulated depreciation		19,800		
Purchases returns		2,781		
Purchases ledger control account		92,831		
Sales		169,200		
Sales returns	5,421		2,676	
Sales ledger control account	12,569			672
Suspense	3,526			3,526

(b)

Account	Debit ✓	Credit ✓
Allowance for doubtful debts adjustment	134	
Income statement		134
Transfer of allowance for doubtful debts adjustment for year ended 31 December 20X6 to income statement.		

Task 2.4

Extended trial balance

Ledger account	Ledger balances		Adjustments		Income statement		Statement of financial position	
	£	£	£	£	£	£	£	£
Bank	5,246						5,246	
Capital		19,600						19,600
Closing inventory			6,712	6,712		6,712	6,712	
Depreciation charge	4,298		4,000		8,298			
Discounts received		2,291		1,325		3,616		
Drawings	11,712		9,826				21,538	
Irrecoverable debts	627				627			
Motor expenses	2,065				2,065			
Motor vehicles accumulated depreciation		12,500		4,000				16,500
Motor vehicles at cost	20,000						20,000	
Office expenses	7,219				7,219			
Opening inventory	4,820				4,820			
Purchases	91,289				91,289			
Purchases ledger control account		7,109	786					6,323
Salaries	32,781		3,484		36,265			
Sales		156,782				156,782		
Sales ledger control account	11,092						11,092	
Suspense	12,771		1,325	14,096				
VAT		5,638						5,638
					16,527			16,527
	203,920	203,920	26,133	26,133	167,110	167,110	64,588	64,588

Task 2.5

Adjustment	Amount £	Debit ✓	Credit ✓
Adjustment for 1	1,489	✓	
Adjustment for 2	1,267	✓	
Adjustment for 4	180		✓

Task 2.6

✓	
	Credit the allowance for doubtful debts account
	Debit the irrecoverable debts account
✓	Credit the allowance for doubtful debts adjustment account
	Credit the sales ledger control account
	None of the above

BPP PRACTICE ASSESSMENT 3
ACCOUNTS PREPARATION I

Time allowed: 2 hours

Section 1

Task 1.1

This task is about recording information for non-current assets for a business known as Tilling Brothers. The business is registered for VAT and its year end is 31 December.

The following is a purchase invoice received by Tilling Brothers:

Prestatyn Machinery Ltd 82 Main Road Perwith PE5 9LA	Invoice 654723	Date:	1 May 20X3
To:	Tilling Brothers 56 Kerrick Street Perwith PE4 7PA		
Description	Item number	Quantity	£
Press machine	MAC637	1	8,640.00
Delivery and set-up charges		1	300.00
Maintenance pack (1 year)		1	184.00
Net			9,124.00
VAT @ 20%			1,824.80
Total			10,948.80
Settlement terms: strictly 30 days net.			

The following information relates to the sale of a computer:

Identification number	COM265
Date of sale	1 January 20X3
Selling price excluding VAT	£850.00

- Tilling Brothers' policy is to recognise items of capital expenditure over £200 as non-current assets.

- Machinery is depreciated at 25% using the straight line method with a full year's charge in the year of purchase and none in the year of sale.

- Computer equipment is depreciated at 30% per annum using the reducing balance method.

Record the following information in the non-current assets register below:

(a) Any acquisitions of non-current assets during the year ended 31 December 20X3

(b) Any disposals of non-current assets during the year ended 31 December 20X3

(c) Depreciation for the year ended 31 December 20X3

Non-current assets register

Description	Acquisition date	Cost £	Depreciation £	Carrying amount £	Funding method	Disposal proceeds £	Disposal date
Computer equipment							
COM265							
Year end 31/12/X1	1/1/X1	5,600.00	1,680.00	3,920.00	Credit		
Year end 31/12/X2			1,176.00	2,744.00			
Year end 31/12/X3							
COM399					Credit		
Year end 31/12/X2	1/1/X2	7,200.00	2,160.00	5,040.00			
Year end 31/12/X3							
Machinery							
MAC434							
Year end 31/12/X1	1/7/X1	12,940.00	3,235.00	9,705.00	Credit		
Year end 31/12/X2			3,235.00	6,470.00			
Year end 31/12/X3							
Year end 31/12/X3							

Task 1.2

This task is about recording non-current asset information in the general ledger and other non-current asset matters.

- You are working on the accounts of a business which is not registered for VAT. The business's year end is 31 December 20X3.

- On 1 January 20X3 the business part exchanged an old machine for a new one with a list price of £3,500. A cheque for £1,000 was paid in full and final settlement and this amount has already been entered in the cash book.

- The old machine cost £4,000 on 1 January 20X1.

- The business's depreciation policy for machinery is 20% using the reducing balance method.

(a) **Make entries to account for the disposal of the old machine and acquisition of the new one.**

   On each account, show clearly the balance carried down or transferred to the income statement.

Machines at cost

	£		£
Balance b/d	12,500		

Machines accumulated depreciation

	£		£
		Balance b/d	4,500

Disposal account

	£		£

(b) **When a non-current asset is acquired by paying a regular monthly amount over a set period and then having ownership transferred at the end of that period, the funding method is described as:**

✓	
	Cash purchase
	Hire purchase
	Borrowing
	Part exchange

Section 2

Task 2.1

This task is about accounting for accruals and prepayments and preparing a trial balance.

You are working on the final accounts of a business for the year ended 31 December 20X3. In this task, you can ignore VAT.

You have the following information:

Balances as at:	1 January 20X3 £
Accrual of rental income	1,000
Accrual of heat and light	345

The bank summary for the year shows receipts of rental income of £3,750. This included rent of £500 for January 20X4.

(a) **Prepare the rental income account for the year ended 31 December 20X3 and close it off by showing the transfer to the income statement.**

Rental income

Details	£	Details	£

The bank summary for the year shows payments for heat and light of £4,670. In February 20X4, an invoice for £1,290 was received in respect of the quarter ended 31 January 20X4.

(b) **Prepare the heat and light account for the year ended 31 December 20X3 and close it off by showing the transfer to the income statement. Include dates.**

Heat and light

Date	Details	£	Date	Details	£

Task 2.2

This task is about preparing a trial balance.

You are working on the accounts of a business with a year end of 31 December. You have five extracts from the ledger accounts as at 31 December 20X3. You need to start preparing the trial balance as at 31 December 20X3.

Using all the information given below and the figures given in the table, enter amounts in the appropriate trial balance columns for the accounts shown.

Do NOT enter zeros in unused column cells.

Do NOT enter any figures as negatives.

Bank

		£			£
31/12/X3	Balance b/f	5,635			

Sundry income

		£			£
			31/12/X3	Balance b/f	1,050

This balance has been adjusted for prepaid income of £125 as at 31/12/X3.

Administration costs

		£			£
31/12/X3	Balance b/f	6,940			

This balance has been adjusted for prepaid expenses of £720 as at 31/12/X3.

VAT

		£			£
			31/03/X7	Balance b/f	4,473

Extract from trial balance as at 31 December 20X3

Account	£	Debit £	Credit £
Accrued expenses			
Accrued income			
Capital	7,300		
Sales returns	456		
Bank			
Sundry income			
Administration costs			
VAT			
Prepaid expenses			
Prepaid income			

••

Task 2.3

This task is about recording adjustments in the extended trial balance and closing off accounts.

You are working on the final accounts of a business with a year end of 31 December 20X3. A trial balance has been drawn up and a suspense account opened with a debit balance of £1,772. You now need to make some corrections and adjustments for the year ended 31 December 20X3.

(a) **Record the adjustments needed on the extract from the extended trial balance to deal with the items below.**

You will not need to enter adjustments on every line. Do NOT enter zeros into unused cells.

(i) An allowance for doubtful debts of £2,420 is required at the year end.

(ii) A total column of £1,560 in the purchases returns day book was credited to the purchases ledger control account. All the other entries were made correctly

(iii) Closing inventory for the year end 31 December 20X3 has not yet been recorded. Its value at cost is £12,860. Included in this figure are some items costing £1,250 that will be sold for £1,140.

(iv) A contra for £674 was debited to both the sales ledger control account and the purchases ledger control account.

Extract from extended trial balance

	Ledger balances		Adjustments	
	Debit £	Credit £	Debit £	Credit £
Allowance for doubtful debts adjustment				
Allowance for doubtful debts		2,563		
Closing inventory – SFP				
Closing inventory – income statement				
Bank overdraft		265		
Irrecoverable debts				
Purchases	567,239			
Purchases returns		8,922		
Purchases ledger control account		81,272		
Sales		926,573		
Sales returns	4,982			
Sales ledger control account	109,282			
Suspense	1,772			

(b) **The ledgers are ready to be closed off for the year ended 31 December 20X3. Show the correct entries to close off the sales returns account and insert an appropriate narrative.**

Account	Debit ✓	Credit ✓

Task 2.4

This task is about completing an extended trial balance.

You have the following extended trial balance. The adjustments have already been correctly entered.

Extend the figures into the income statement and statement of financial position columns.

Do NOT enter zeros into unused column cells.

Make the columns balance by entering figures and a label in the correct places.

Extended trial balance

Ledger account	Ledger balances		Adjustments		Income statement		Statement of financial position	
	£	£	£	£	£	£	£	£
Bank	7,281						7,281	
Capital		152,600						152,600
Closing inventory			15,729	15,729		15,729	15,729	
Depreciation charge			27,600		27,600			
Commission income		18,272		3,825		22,097		
Drawings	40,000						40,000	
Accrued income			3,825				3,825	
Prepaid expenses			1,427				1,427	
Motor vehicles accumulated depreciation		88,900		27,600				116,500
Motor vehicles at cost	170,000		4,300				174,300	
General expenses	67,298			1,427	65,871			
Opening inventory	17,268				17,268			
Purchases	98,245			726	97,519			
Purchases ledger control account		14,681	710					13,971
Salaries	69,256				69,256			
Sales		201,675				201,675		
Sales ledger control account	17,504			710			16,794	
Suspense	3,574		726	4,300				
VAT		14,298						14,298
Loss for the year						38,013	38,013	
	490,426	490,426	54,317	54,317	277,514	277,514	297,369	297,369

Task 2.5

This task is about preparing reconciliations.

The bank statement has been compared with the cash book and the following differences identified:

1   Bank charges of £121 were not entered in the cash book.

2   A cheque received from a customer for £280 has been recorded in the cash receipts book but it has been dishonoured and this has not yet been entered in the records.

3   A cheque for £765 to a supplier has not yet been presented for payment at the bank.

4   A direct debit of £650 to the local council appears only on the bank statement.

The balance showing on the bank statement is a debit of £660 and the balance in the cash book is a credit of £374.

Use the following table to show the THREE adjustments you need to make to the cash book.

Adjustment	Amount £	Debit ✓	Credit ✓

Task 2.6

This task is to test your knowledge. Choose ONE answer.

When the cash book operates only as a book of prime entry there is a ledger account for Bank in the general ledger to which total receipts and payments are posted.

✓	
	True
	False

BPP PRACTICE ASSESSMENT 3
ACCOUNTS PREPARATION I

ANSWERS

Section 1

Task 1.1

(a)-(c)

Non-current assets register

Description	Acquisition date	Cost £	Depreciation £	Carrying amount £	Funding method	Disposal proceeds £	Disposal date
Computer equipment							
COM265							
Year end 31/12/X1	1/1/X1	5,600.00	1,680.00	3,920.00	Credit		
Year end 31/12/X2			1,176.00	2,744.00			
Year end 31/12/X3						850.00	1/1/X3
COM399					Credit		
Year end 31/12/X2	1/1/X2	7,200.00	2,160.00	5,040.00			
Year end 31/12/X3			**1,512.00**	**3,528.00**			
Machinery							
MAC434							
Year end 31/12/X1	1/7/X1	12,940.00	3,235.00	9,705.00	Credit		
Year end 31/12/X2			3,235.00	6,470.00			
Year end 31/12/X3			**3,235.00**	**3,235.00**			
MAC637	**1/5/X3**	**8,940.00**					
Year end 31/12/X3			**2,235.00**	**6,705.00**			

BPP LEARNING MEDIA

Task 1.2

(a)

Machines at cost

	£		£
Balance b/d	12,500	Disposal account	4,000
Bank	1,000	Balance c/d	12,000
Part-exchange allowance	2,500		
	16,000		16,000

Machines accumulated depreciation

	£		£
Disposals account	1,440	Balance b/d	4,500
Balance c/d	3,060		
	4,500		4,500

Disposal account

	£		£
Machines at cost	4,000	Part exchange allowance	2,500
		Machines accumulated depreciation	1,440
		Income statement	60
	4,000		4,000

(b)

✓	
	Cash purchase
✓	Hire purchase
	Borrowing
	Part exchange

Section 2

Task 2.1

(a)

Rental income

Details	£	Details	£
Balance b/d	1,000	Bank	3,750
Balance c/d	500		
Income statement	2,250		
	3,750		3,750

(b)

Heat and light

Date	Details	£	Date	Details	£
31/12	Balance c/d	860	1/1	Balance b/d	345
31/12	Bank	4,670	31/12	Income statement	5,185
		5,530			5,530

Task 2.2

Extract from trial balance as at 31 December 20X3

Account	£	Debit £	Credit £
Accrued expenses			
Accrued income			
Capital	7,300		7,300
Sales returns	456	456	
Bank		5,635	
Sundry income			1,050
Administration costs		6,940	
VAT			4,473
Prepaid expenses		720	
Prepaid income			125

Task 2.3

(a)

Extract from extended trial balance

	Ledger balances		Adjustments	
	Debit £	Credit £	Debit £	Credit £
Allowance for doubtful debts adjustment				143
Allowance for doubtful debts		2,563	143	
Closing inventory – SFP			12,750	
Closing inventory – income statement				12,750
Bank overdraft		265		
Irrecoverable debts				
Purchases	567,239			
Purchases returns		8,922		
Purchases ledger control account		81,272	3,120	
Sales		926,573		
Sales returns	4,982			
Sales ledger control account	109,282			1,348
Suspense	1,772		1,348	3,120

(b)

Account	Debit ✓	Credit ✓
Income statement	✓	
Sales returns		✓
Transfer of sales returns for year ended 31 December 20X3 to income statement		

Task 2.4

Extended trial balance

Ledger account	Ledger balances		Adjustments		Income statement		Statement of financial position	
	£	£	£	£	£	£	£	£
Bank	7,281						7,281	
Capital		152,600						152,600
Closing inventory			15,729	15,729		15,729	15,729	
Depreciation charge			27,600		27,600			
Commission income		18,272		3,825		22,097		
Drawings	40,000						40,000	
Accrued income			3,825				3,825	
Prepaid expenses			1,427				1,427	
Motor vehicles accumulated depreciation		88,900		27,600				116,500
Motor vehicles at cost	170,000		4,300				174,300	
General expenses	67,298			1,427	65,871			
Opening inventory	17,268				17,268			
Purchases	98,245			726	97,519			
Purchases ledger control account		14,681	710					13,971
Salaries	69,256				69,256			
Sales		201,675				201,675		
Sales ledger control account	17,504			710			16,794	
Suspense	3,574		726	4,300				
VAT		14,298						14,298
Net loss						38,013	38,013	
	490,426	490,426	54,317	54,317	**277,514**	**277,514**	**297,369**	**297,369**

Task 2.5

Adjustment	Amount £	Debit ✓	Credit ✓
Adjustment for 1	121		✓
Adjustment for 2	280		✓
Adjustment for 4	650		✓

Task 2.6

✓	
✓	True
	False

....

BPP PRACTICE ASSESSMENT 4
ACCOUNTS PREPARATION I

Time allowed: 2 hours

Section 1

Task 1.1

This task is about recording information for non-current assets for a business known as Markham Ltd. The business is registered for VAT and its year end is 30 June.

The following is a purchase invoice received by Markham Ltd:

Office Solutions Ltd Unit 7 Tenton Industrial Estate TN14 5YJ	Invoice 9746	Date:	1 March 20X3
To:	Markham Ltd 14 The Green Tenton TN3 4ZX		
Description	Item number	Quantity	£
Corner office suite	OF477	1	1,950.00
Delivery and assembly charges		1	150.00
Printer ink cartridges		20	160.00
Net			2,260.00
VAT @ 20%			452.00
Total			2,712.00
Settlement terms: strictly 30 days net.			

The following information relates to the sale of an item of factory machinery:

Identification number	MN864
Date of sale	1 January 20X3
Selling price excluding VAT	£1,050.00

- Markham Ltd's policy is to recognise items of capital expenditure over £500 as non-current assets.

- Office equipment and furniture is depreciated at 20% per annum using the straight line method. There are no residual values.

- Factory machinery is depreciated at 25% per annum using the reducing balance method.

A full year's depreciation is charged in the year of acquisition and none in the year of sale.

Record the following information in the non-current assets register below:

(a) **Any acquisitions of non-current assets during the year ended 30 June 20X3**
(b) **Any disposals of non-current assets during the year ended 30 June 20X3**
(c) **Depreciation for the year ended 30 June 20X3**

Non-current assets register

Description	Acquisition date	Cost £	Depreciation £	Carrying amount £	Funding method	Disposal proceeds £	Disposal date
Factory machinery							
MN864	01/02/X1	15,600.00					
Year end 30/06/X1			3,900.00	11,700.00	Credit		
Year end 30/06/X2			2,925.00	8,775.00			
Year end 30/06/X3							
MN982	01/01/X2	9,400.00			Credit		
Year end 30/06/X2			2,350.00	7,050.00			
Year end 30/06/X3							
Office equipment							
OF025	01/04/X1	12,940.00					
Year end 30/06/X1			2,588.00	10,352.00	Credit		
Year end 30/06/X2			2,588.00	7,764.00			
Year end 30/06/X3							
Year end 30/06/X3							

Task 1.2

This task is about recording non-current asset information in the general ledger and other non-current asset matters.

- You are working on the accounts of a business that is registered for VAT. The business's year end is 31 December 20XX.

- On 1 September 20XX the business bought a new motor vehicle costing £15,000 excluding VAT.

- The vehicle's residual value is expected to be £3,000 excluding VAT.

- The business's depreciation policy for motor vehicles is 20% per annum on a straight line basis.

- Depreciation has already been entered into the accounts for the business's existing motor vehicles.

Make entries to account for:

(a) **The purchase of the new motor vehicle**
(b) **The depreciation on the new motor vehicle**

On each account, show clearly the balance carried down or transferred to the income statement.

Motor vehicles at cost

	£		£
Balance b/d	35,000		

Motor vehicles accumulated depreciation

	£		£
		Balance b/d	9,400

Depreciation charge

	£		£
Balance b/d	6,300		

(c) When non-current assets are depreciated using the straight line method, an equal amount is charged for each year of the asset's life.

✓	
	True
	False

Section 2

Task 2.1

This task is about accounting for accruals and prepayments and preparing a trial balance.

You are working on the final accounts of a business for the year ended 31 December 20X3. In this task, you can ignore VAT.

You have the following information:

Balances as at:	1 January 20X3
	£
Accrual of rental income	2,100
Accrual of selling expenses	1,445

The bank summary for the year shows receipts of rental income of £4,850. This included rent of £600 for January 20X4.

(a) **Prepare the rental income account for the year ended 31 December 20X3 and close it off by showing the transfer to the income statement.**

Rental income

Details	£	Details	£

The bank summary for the year shows payments for selling expenses of £5,770. In February 20X4, an invoice for £2,385 was received in respect of the quarter ended 31 January 20X4.

(b) **Prepare the selling expenses account for the year ended 31 December 20X3 and close it off by showing the transfer to the income statement. Include dates.**

Selling expenses

Date	Details	£	Date	Details	£

Task 2.2

This task is about preparing a trial balance.

You are working on the accounts of a business with a year end of 31 December. You have five extracts from the ledger accounts as at 31 December 20X3. You need to start preparing the trial balance as at 31 December 20X3.

Using all the information given below and the figures given in the table, enter amounts in the appropriate trial balance columns for the accounts shown.

Do NOT enter zeros in unused column cells.

Do NOT enter any figures as negatives.

Allowance for doubtful debts adjustment

		£		£
31/12/X3	Balance b/f	660		

Disposal of non-current asset

		£			£
			31/12/X3	Balance b/f	1,200

Office costs

		£		£
31/12/X3	Balance b/f	2,950		

Included in this balance is an amount for accrued expenses of £570 as at 31/12/X3.

Recycling rebates

		£			£
			31/12/X3	Balance b/f	3,560

Included in this balance is an amount for accrued income of £250 as at 31/12/X3.

VAT

		£			£
			31/12/X3	Balance b/f	1,222

Extract from trial balance as at 31 December 20X3

Account	£	Debit £	Credit £
Accrued expenses			
Accrued income			
Purchases returns	8,400		
Discounts allowed	1,556		
Discounts received	2,027		
Allowance for doubtful debts adjustment			
Disposal of non-current asset			
Office costs			
Recycling rebates			
VAT			
Prepaid expenses			
Prepaid income			

Task 2.3

This task is about recording adjustments in the extended trial balance and closing off accounts.

You are the accountant preparing the final accounts of a business with a year end of 31 December 20X5. A trial balance has been drawn up and a suspense account opened with a debit balance of £2,098. You now need to make some corrections and adjustments for the year ended 31 December 20X5.

(a) **Record the adjustments needed on the extract from the extended trial balance to deal with the items below.**

You will not need to enter adjustments on every line. Do NOT enter zeros into unused cells.

(i) An allowance for doubtful debts of £3,200 is required at the year end.

(ii) A total column of £1,885 in the purchases returns day book was credited to the purchases ledger control account. All the other entries were made correctly

(iii) Closing inventory for the year end 31 December 20X5 has not yet been recorded. Its value at cost is £13,185. Included in this figure are some items costing £1,575 that will be sold for £1,400.

(iv) A contra for £836 was debited to both the sales ledger control account and the purchases ledger control account.

Extract from extended trial balance

	Ledger balances		Adjustments	
	Debit £	Credit £	Debit £	Credit £
Allowance for doubtful debts adjustment				
Allowance for doubtful debts		2,888		
Closing inventory – SFP				
Closing inventory – income statement				
Bank overdraft		590		
Irrecoverable debts				
Purchases	675,564			
Purchases returns		9,247		
Purchases ledger control account		92,597		
Sales		843,898		
Sales returns	5,307			
Sales ledger control account	98,607			
Suspense	2,098			

(b) **The ledgers are ready to be closed off for the year ended 31 December 20X5. Show the correct entries to close off the purchases returns account and insert an appropriate narrative.**

Account	Debit ✓	Credit ✓

Task 2.4

This task is about completing an extended trial balance.

You have the following extended trial balance. The adjustments have already been correctly entered.

Extend the figures into the income statement and statement of financial position columns.

Do NOT enter zeros into unused column cells.

Make the columns balance by entering figures and a label in the correct places.

Extended trial balance

Ledger account	Ledger balances £	Ledger balances £	Adjustments £	Adjustments £	Income statement £	Income statement £	Statement of financial position £	Statement of financial position £
Machinery at cost	200,000		3,400				203,400	
Machinery accumulated depreciation		125,000		14,600				139,600
Closing inventory			9,433	9,433		9,433	9,433	
Sales ledger control account	25,775			399			25,376	
Accrued income			249				249	
Prepaid expenses			765				765	
Bank	7,281						7,281	
Capital		150,000						150,000
Drawings	10,000						10,000	
Purchases ledger control account		17,493	399					17,094
VAT		8,965						8,965
Sales		195,433				195,433		
Opening inventory	13,254				13,254			
Purchases	128,994			2,458	126,536			
Commission income		7,893		249		8,142		
Salaries	75,606				75,606			
General expenses	42,932			765	42,167			
Depreciation charge			14,600		14,600			
Suspense	942		2,458	3,400				
Loss for the year						59,155	59,155	
	504,784	504,784	31,304	31,304	272,163	272,163	315,659	315,659

Task 2.5

This task is about preparing reconciliations.

The bank statement has been compared with the cash book and the following differences identified:

1   A standing order of £269 has not been entered in the cash book.

2   A cheque received from a customer for £500 has been recorded in the cash receipts book but the bank has informed us that the cheque was subsequently dishonoured.

3   A cheque for £940 to a supplier has not yet been presented for payment at the bank.

4   A direct debit of £485 to an utility company appears only on the bank statement.

The balance showing on the bank statement is a debit of £890 and the balance in the cash book is a credit of £576.

Use the following table to show the THREE adjustments you need to make to the cash book.

Adjustment	Amount £	Debit ✓	Credit ✓

....

Task 2.6

This task is to test your knowledge. Choose ONE answer.

A debit balance on the cash book means that the business has funds available

✓	
	True
	False

....

BPP PRACTICE ASSESSMENT 4
ACCOUNTS PREPARATION I

ANSWERS

Section 1

Task 1.1

(a)-(c)

Non-current assets register

Description	Acquisition date	Cost £	Depreciation £	Carrying amount £	Funding method	Disposal proceeds £	Disposal date
Factory machinery							
MN864	01/02/X1	15,600.00					
Year end 30/06/X1			3,900.00	11,700.00	Credit		
Year end 30/06/X2			2,925.00	8,775.00			
Year end 30/06/X3						1,050.00	01/01/X3
MN982	01/01/X2	9,400.00			Credit		
Year end 30/06/X2			2,350.00	7,050.00			
Year end 30/06/X3			1,762.50	5,287.50			
Office equipment							
OF025	01/04/X1	12,940.00					
Year end 30/06/X1			2,588.00	10,352.00	Credit		
Year end 30/06/X2			2,588.00	7,764.00			
Year end 30/06/X3			25,888.00	5,176.00			
OF477	01/03/X3	2,100.00					
Year end 30/06/X3			420.00	1,680.00			

Task 1.2

(a) and (b)

Motor vehicles at cost

	£		£
Balance b/d	35,000	Balance c/d	50,000
Purchases ledger control	15,000		
	50,000		50,000

Motor vehicles accumulated depreciation

	£		£
Balance c/d	11,800	Balance b/d	9,400
		Depreciation charge	2,400
	11,800		11,800

Depreciation charge

	£		£
Balance b/d	6,300	Income statement	8,700
Motor vehicles accumulated depreciation	2,400		
	8,700		8,700

(c)

✓	
✓	True
	False

Section 2

Task 2.1

(a)

Rental income

Details	£	Details	£
Balance b/d	2,100	Bank	4,850
Balance c/d	600		
Income statement	2,150		
	4,850		4,850

(b)

Selling expenses

Date	Details	£	Date	Details	£
31/12	Bank	5,770	1/1	Balance b/d	1,445
31/12	Balance c/d	1,590	31/12	Income statement	5,915
		7,360			7,360

Task 2.2

Extract from trial balance as at 31 December 20X3

Account	£	Debit £	Credit £
Accrued expenses			570
Accrued income		250	
Purchases returns	8,400		8,400
Discounts allowed	1,556	1,556	
Discounts received	2,027		2,027
Allowance for doubtful debts adjustment		660	
Disposal of non-current asset			1,200
Office costs		2,950	
Recycling rebates			3,560
VAT			1,222
Prepaid expenses			
Prepaid income			

Task 2.3

(a)

Extract from extended trial balance

	Ledger balances		Adjustments	
	Debit	Credit	Debit	Credit
	£	£	£	£
Allowance for doubtful debts adjustment			312	
Allowance for doubtful debts		2,888		312
Closing inventory – SFP			13,010	
Closing inventory – income statement				13,010
Bank overdraft		590		
Irrecoverable debts				
Purchases	675,564			
Purchases returns		9,247		
Purchases ledger control account		92,597	3,770	
Sales		843,898		
Sales returns	5,307			
Sales ledger control account	98,607			1,672
Suspense	2,098		1,672	3,770

(b)

Account	Debit ✓	Credit ✓
Purchases returns	✓	
Income statement		✓
Transfer of purchases returns for year ended 31 December 20X5 to income statement		

Task 2.4

Extended trial balance

Ledger account	Ledger balances		Adjustments		Income statement		Statement of financial position	
	£	£	£	£	£	£	£	£
Machinery at cost	200,000		3,400				203,400	
Machinery accumulated depreciation		125,000		14,600				139,600
Closing inventory			9,433	9,433		9,433	9,433	
Sales ledger control account	25,775			399			25,376	
Accrued income			249				249	
Prepaid expenses			765				765	
Bank	7,281						7,281	
Capital		150,000						150,000
Drawings	10,000						10,000	
Purchases ledger control account		17,493	399					17,094
VAT		8,965						8,965
Sales		195,433				195,433		
Opening inventory	13,254				13,254			
Purchases	128,994			2,458	126,536			
Commission income		7,893		249		8,142		
Salaries	75,606				75,606			
General expenses	42,932			765	42,167			
Depreciation charge			14,600		14,600			
Suspense	942		2,458	3,400				
Net loss						59,155	59,155	
	504,784	504,784	31,304	31,304	272,163	272,163	315,659	315,659

Task 2.5

Adjustment	Amount £	Debit ✓	Credit ✓
Adjustment for 1	269		✓
Adjustment for 2	500		✓
Adjustment for 4	485		✓

Task 2.6

✓	
✓	True
	False

....

Notes

Notes

Notes

Notes

Notes

Notes

Notes